Fiji

Cultural Awareness and Business Negotiations

Country Study

Contents

Introduction...

1. What is Culture? ....

2. Country Overview ....

3. Core Values and Beliefs ....

4. Customes and Traditons............................

5. Communication Styles ....

6. Business Etiquette ....

7. Social Etiquette...

8. Body Language and Personal Space ....

9. Education and the Arts ....

10. Practical Tips for Travellers and Expats .....

11. Overcoming Stereotypes ....

12. Building Cross-Cultural Relationships ....

13. Case Studies and Real Life Examples ....

INTRODUCTION

In our increasingly interconnected world, understanding and embracing cultural diversity has become essential for both personal and professional success. This series of Cultural Awareness books aims to provide participants with the knowledge, skills, and tools necessary to better understand and navigate various cultural contexts. By investing in cultural awareness, we are not only fostering stronger relationships but also paving the way for more successful business ventures and personal growth.

The expanding Global market presents immense opportunities for businesses. However, these opportunities come with the responsibility of understanding the nuances of various cultures. Unintentional cultural misunderstandings can jeopardise your chances of securing a crucial foothold in this lucrative market. This series highlights the importance of being aware of cultural differences and equips you with the tools to deal with the challenges that may arise when interacting with individuals from different cultural backgrounds.

Individuals and families who have travelled or are planning to move to different countries also face the challenge of adapting to new cultures. Culture shock can be overwhelming if one is not prepared to handle the changes that come with relocating. This course offers practical insights and tools to help individuals and families better understand and navigate the complexities of their new cultural environment.

Cultural awareness goes beyond learning facts or memorizing customs; it is about cultivating a genuine appreciation for the richness of human experiences. This series encourages participants to look beyond their own cultural lens and develop empathy for the perspectives of others. By doing so, we foster a more inclusive and harmonious world where people from diverse backgrounds can come together and create meaningful connections.

Throughout this book, you will be introduced to various cultural frameworks, practices, and traditions, as well as common misconceptions and stereotypes that often contribute to misunderstandings and miscommunications. Engaging with these topics will enable you to recognise cultural differences, appreciate their value, and navigate them effectively.

In conclusion, cultural awareness is essential for anyone aiming to expand their reach in the global market, adapt to new cultural environments, or enrich their lives by embracing the beauty of human diversity. By undertaking this journey, you are taking a significant step toward creating a more inclusive, empathetic, and successful future.

Ask yourself: Can you afford to miss out on the vital opportunities and personal growth that cultural awareness can bring to your life? The time to invest in cultural understanding is now. Welcome to an enlightening and transformative journey.

1. WHAT IS CULTURE?

What is Culture?

The Culture of a people can be understood as the system of shared ideas and meanings, explicit and implicit, which a people use to interpret the world, and which serve to pattern their behaviour.

This includes an understanding of the art, literature, and history of a society, but also less tangible aspects such as attitudes, prejudices, folklore etc. Unconscious or conscious habits are just as important as art and history.

Values - What people say one ought to do or not do? What is considered good or bad - the importance of honesty, or chastity?

Laws - What political authorities have decided people should do, and what the sanctions are?

Rules - What a society has decided its members should do. Social rules about marriage ages, childrearing.

Social Categories- Ways of thinking about people as types. - "friends", "criminals", "lovers", "nobles", "clergy".

Tacit Models - Implicit standards and patterns of behaviour that a person does not think about - knowing how to address a police officer rather than friends. Knowing how to dress for a job interview as opposed to a dance.

Fundamental - Categories and ways of thinking that people take for granted and may not recognise even when pointed out. - thinking in dualities good/bad, male/female.

Culture shapes

- The way we think
- The way we interact
- The way we communicate
- The way we transmit knowledge to the next generation

Culture manifests itself in

- Food
- Religion
- Dress
- Differences in language
- Our expectations of male and female roles
- Non-verbal rules and body language

The first step is in understanding the values and rules for behaviour of our own culture - the "normal" or "right" way of doing things. What makes us different?

Geert Hofstede

Between 1967 and 1973 Geert Hofstede conducted a study on culture across 100 000 employees of IBM in 50 countries. From this he developed a framework to 'measure' the 'value dimensions' of various cultures.

Hofstede identified 4 values which can be related to each culture:

- Individualism
- Masculinity
- Power Distance, and
- Uncertainty Avoidance

Later studies by Trompenaar have added several more; however, I will address the 4 basic values along with one later addition relating to time.

From surveys, Hofstede was able to map the cultures and compare them, and from this extrapolate as to why a culture may act in a particular way.

Taking the basic values separately, measured on a scale of 0 to 100.

	ID	M	PD	UA	LT
AUS	90H	61H	38M	51M	21L
FJI	14L	46M	78H	48M	-

H = top third of countries

M = medium

L = bottom third

Individualism v. Collectivism

This dimension aims to measure the degree of interdependence among members of a society and how they define their self-image.

In <u>individualistic</u> societies:

- People prioritize their personal goals, needs, and achievements over those of their social groups.
- Independence and self-reliance are highly valued, and people are encouraged to express their individual opinions and preferences.
- Personal success and accomplishments are celebrated, and competition is often seen as a driving force for progress.
- Relationships tend to be more flexible, and people have the freedom to choose their own social circles and affiliations.
- The primary responsibility of individuals is to take care of themselves and their immediate family members.

In **collectivist** societies:

- The welfare of the group is placed above individual interests, and people are expected to contribute to the success and well-being of their social groups.
- Interdependence and cooperation are highly valued, and individuals are expected to conform to the norms and expectations of their group.
- Social harmony and group cohesion are prioritized, with conflict resolution often focused on finding a compromise that benefits the group as a whole.
- Relationships tend to be more stable, and people are born into strong, tight-knit social groups that provide support and protection throughout their lives.
- Loyalty to one's 'in-group' is paramount, and individuals are expected to prioritize the needs of their group over their own.

The distinction between individualism and collectivism reflects the ways in which societies balance individual autonomy and group harmony. It is important to note that these dimensions are not mutually exclusive; rather, they represent a spectrum along which different cultures fall. Understanding these cultural differences can help in navigating cross-cultural communication and collaboration effectively.

Fiji's low score of **14** in individualism-collectivism dimension indicates that it is indeed a highly collectivistic society. Collectivist cultures place a strong emphasis on group identity, social harmony, and maintaining close relationships within their community. Here are some key aspects of collectivist societies like Fiji:

Group orientation: In collectivist societies, people prioritize the needs and goals of their group (family, extended family, or other social groups) over their own individual needs and aspirations. The welfare of the group is considered more important than personal achievements.

Interdependence: Members of collectivist societies rely heavily on one another for emotional and practical support. They tend to form strong bonds with their group members and are expected to aid when needed.

Loyalty: Loyalty towards one's group is considered a crucial virtue in collectivist cultures. Individuals are expected to stand by their group members, even if it means sacrificing their personal interests or breaking societal rules.

Saving face: In collectivist societies, maintaining one's reputation and avoiding shame or embarrassment is important. People are expected to avoid actions that could bring shame or discredit to their group.

Family and workplace dynamics: In collectivist societies like Fiji, family and workplace relationships often overlap. Employers and employees may view their working relationships in moral terms, similar to family bonds. Hiring and promotion decisions may consider an employee's connections with their in-group, rather than solely focusing on their individual qualifications or merit.

Conflict resolution: Collectivist societies place a high value on social harmony and avoiding direct confrontation. Conflict resolution may involve finding a compromise that benefits the group as a whole, rather than addressing individual concerns.

Group decision-making: Decisions are often made collectively, with input from all group members, rather than being left to an individual. This can lead to a slower decision-making process, but it ensures that everyone's opinions and concerns are considered.

Overall, Fiji's collectivist culture emphasizes the importance of strong relationships, loyalty, and group harmony. These values are deeply ingrained in various aspects of the society, from family life to workplace dynamics.

Masculinity v. Femininity

This dimension measures the dominant values in a society and the extent to which they prioritize competition, achievement, and material success (masculine) versus caring for others, quality of life, and work-life balance (feminine).

Fiji has an intermediate score of **46** in this dimension, which suggests a mix of both Masculine and Feminine values within the society. This means that Fijian culture may exhibit some characteristics from both ends of the spectrum, and cultural preferences could vary depending on the context or specific situations.

In a society with mixed Masculine and Feminine values like Fiji, you may observe the following:

Balance between competition and cooperation: People might be motivated by both personal success and the well-being of their community or workplace. They may strive for achievement while also valuing collaboration and support for others.

Flexible gender roles: The society might not have strictly defined roles for men and women. Both men and women may be encouraged to pursue careers and contribute to the family or community, and both may be expected to demonstrate empathy and care for others.

Emphasis on quality of life: While material success and achievements might be valued, there could also be a strong emphasis on personal well-being, work-life balance, and enjoying the simple pleasures of life.

Context-dependent motivation: People's motivation and priorities might change depending on the context, with some situations emphasizing competitive success and others focusing on personal satisfaction and enjoying one's work.

In summary, with an intermediate score in the Masculinity vs. Femininity dimension, Fiji's culture may display a blend of both competitive and nurturing values. This can lead to a diverse and adaptable society, where people's motivations and priorities can vary depending on the situation and individual preferences.

Power Distance

This dimension measures the extent to which a society accepts and expects unequal distribution of power and authority within its institutions and organizations.

With a high score of **78**, Fiji exhibits a high power distance culture, which is characterised by:

Hierarchy: People in Fiji generally accept a hierarchical social order, where individuals have different levels of authority and status based on their position or role within society. This hierarchical structure is perceived as natural and does not require further justification.

Centralisation: Decision-making in organisations is often centralised, with top-level management making most of the decisions. This can result in less delegation of authority and fewer opportunities for subordinates to participate in decision-making processes.

Respect for authority: Subordinates in high power distance cultures like Fiji expect to be told what to do by their superiors and may not question or challenge their decisions. There is a general understanding that those in higher positions possess more knowledge and expertise.

Benevolent autocracy: In Fiji, the ideal boss is often seen as a benevolent autocrat, someone who makes decisions for the greater good of the organisation while also taking care of the needs and well-being of their subordinates.

Inequality acceptance: People in high power distance societies tend to accept social and economic inequalities as a natural part of life. They may be more comfortable with disparities in wealth, status, and power.

It is essential to understand the power distance dimension when interacting with people from Fiji or other high power distance cultures. Recognizing the value placed on hierarchy, respecting authority, and adapting communication styles accordingly can help in fostering productive cross-cultural relationships.

Uncertainty Avoidance

This dimension reflects the extent to which a society feels threatened by ambiguity or uncertain situations and the strategies they use to cope with this anxiety.

Fiji's relatively low score of **48** on Uncertainty Avoidance indicates that its culture is generally more relaxed and pragmatic in dealing with uncertainty and ambiguity. Some characteristics of low Uncertainty Avoidance cultures like Fiji include:

Flexibility: People in Fiji are more adaptable to change and are willing to adjust their plans as needed. They are more likely to embrace new ideas, technologies, and practices without excessive resistance.

Tolerance for ambiguity: Fijian culture generally accepts that the future is uncertain and embraces the unknown to some extent. People are more comfortable with ambiguity and may not feel the need to have strict rules and regulations to control every aspect of their lives.

Risk-taking: People in low Uncertainty Avoidance societies are more open to taking risks, whether in their personal or professional lives. They may be more entrepreneurial and open to experimenting with new approaches or solutions.

Emotional restraint: Emotions may not be openly expressed or displayed in low Uncertainty Avoidance cultures. People tend to maintain a more relaxed demeanour and may not be overly expressive of their feelings.

Generalists and experts: Both generalists and experts are valued in societies with low Uncertainty Avoidance. Generalists bring adaptability and versatility, while experts contribute their specialised knowledge and skills.

In summary, Fiji's low Uncertainty Avoidance score suggests that its culture is generally more adaptable, tolerant of ambiguity, and open to change. Understanding this aspect of Fijian culture can help in navigating cross-cultural interactions and collaborations more effectively.

Long Term Orientation

This dimension assesses the extent to which societies prioritize long-term goals and future-oriented values as opposed to maintaining traditional norms and values in the short term.

There is no available score for Fiji on this dimension.

Acculturation

Acculturation is the process of adapting to a new culture.

- Variables affecting Acculturation
- The amount of time spent in the process – educating yourself
- The quantity and quality of interaction – trying things

- Ethnicity or nation of origin – how far is it removed from our own
- Affinity – willingness to learn and adapt

Stages of Acculturation

- Acceptance of new culture - honeymoon
- Individual starts to feel comfortable in the new culture
- Feelings of anger, hostility, and frustration
- Recovery
- Culture Shock

Generalisations

We should remember that there will probably never be one person within a culture that actually meets these dimensions. Rather this is a tool to anticipate likely reaction of a particular culture. There is never an average person! What should be remembered is that between the extremes, patterns do exist.

The inverse also applies; do not confuse a particular individual's personality as representative of culture. Whilst Australian's are considered sports loving people, there are people who don't like Rugby – as hard as that is to believe!

Stereotyping – setting a standard idea, concept, or form. This 'notion' has a deeper meaning to our basic survival instincts.

Bias – a particular tendency or preference, which may prevent unprejudiced consideration of a topic. A 'learned' response.

Prejudice - an unfavourable opinion formed beforehand or without knowledge or reason.

Linear and Circular Thinking

How does culture affect Management?

Our Western (Greek) method of teaching & learning is if there is a problem then I can solve it. We are taught to identify issues as a 'problem' that challenges us. The individual works out a plan and overcomes the problem.

In a culture not rooted in the Western traditions, the issue may not be seen as a 'problem'!! Rather it is a divergence or even a side issue that can be avoided or not confronted until a solution is evident

Managing Across Culture

The management theory of MBI (Mapping – Bridging – Integrating) was developed to understand the differences and work out optimum paths to achieve greater workflows.

2. COUNTRY OVERVIEW

History and Geography

Fiji is an archipelago located in the South Pacific Ocean, consisting of over 330 islands, of which around 110 are inhabited. The two largest islands, Viti Levu and Vanua Levu, account for approximately 87% of the country's population. Fiji's capital city is Suva, situated on the south-eastern coast of Viti Levu. The country's total land area is approximately 18,274 square kilometres (7,056 square miles), and it has a population of around 900,000 people.

Brief History

Fiji has a rich history, with human settlement dating back over 3,500 years. The first settlers are believed to have arrived from Southeast Asia, and later, from other parts of the Pacific Islands, particularly Tonga and Samoa. Fijian society developed a complex hierarchical system with numerous chieftaincies and tribal alliances.

European contact with Fiji began in the 17th century, with Dutch explorer Abel Tasman being the first known European to sight the islands in 1643. British explorer Captain James Cook also visited the islands in the 18th century, but it wasn't until the early 19th century that European settlers and missionaries began to establish a presence in Fiji.

In 1874, following a period of internal conflict, Fiji was ceded to the British Empire and became a British Crown Colony. The British introduced a new system of governance and brought in indentured laborers from India to work on sugar plantations. The indentured labour system ended in 1916, and many of the Indian laborers decided to stay in Fiji, creating a diverse multi-ethnic society.

Fiji gained its independence from the United Kingdom on October 10, 1970, and became a member of the British Commonwealth. Since gaining independence, the country has experienced several military coups, mainly due to tensions between the indigenous Fijian and Indo-Fijian communities. In 2014, Fiji held its first democratic elections in eight years, which led to the establishment of a more inclusive and stable government.

Geography

Fiji's islands are mostly of volcanic origin, featuring rugged landscapes, dense tropical rainforests, and mountainous terrain. The highest peak, Mount Tomanivi, stands at 1,324 meters (4,344 feet) on the island of Viti Levu. The islands are surrounded by extensive coral reefs, which provide habitat for a diverse range of marine life and attract tourists for scuba diving and snorkelling.

Fiji has a tropical marine climate, characterized by warm temperatures and high humidity levels. The country experiences a distinct wet season from November to April and a dry season from May to October. Fiji is also prone to natural disasters such as cyclones, floods, and earthquakes due to its location in the Pacific "Ring of Fire."

Political and Economic landscape

Political Landscape

Fiji is a parliamentary republic with a single-chamber parliament consisting of 51 members elected for a four-year term. The President, who serves as the Head of State, is elected by the Parliament for a three-year term. The Prime Minister, as the Head of Government, is appointed by the President and is usually the leader of the party with the majority in Parliament.

Since gaining independence in 1970, Fiji has experienced political instability, with four military coups taking place between 1987 and 2006. These coups were primarily driven by ethnic tensions between the indigenous Fijian and Indo-Fijian communities, as well as disagreements over land rights, political representation, and power dynamics. In 2013, Fiji adopted a new constitution that aimed to address these issues by establishing a more inclusive electoral system and granting equal rights to all citizens, regardless of ethnicity.

The 2014 general election marked Fiji's return to democracy and saw the FijiFirst party, led by Frank Bainimarama (who had been the military commander and later the Prime Minister since the 2006 coup), win a majority of seats in Parliament. Since then, Fiji's political situation has stabilized, and the country has made progress in fostering national unity and promoting inclusive development.

Economic Landscape

Fiji has a small, open economy that is dependent on tourism, agriculture, and remittances from Fijians working overseas. Tourism is the largest industry, accounting for approximately 40% of the country's GDP and employing a significant portion of the workforce. The primary agricultural exports include sugar, coconuts, and fish, while the manufacturing sector focuses on garments, footwear, and food processing.

Fiji has experienced modest economic growth in recent years, driven mainly by the expansion of the tourism industry and increased infrastructure investment. However, the country still faces several economic challenges, such as a lack of diversification, vulnerability to natural disasters, and high levels of public debt.

The government has implemented various reforms aimed at improving the business environment, attracting foreign investment, and promoting economic diversification. Some of these measures include tax incentives for investors, liberalization of trade policies, and investment in infrastructure projects, such as roads, ports, and airports.

Despite the challenges, Fiji remains an important regional hub in the South Pacific due to its strategic location, well-developed infrastructure, and relatively skilled workforce. The country is also a member of various regional and international organizations, such as the Pacific Islands Forum, the World Trade Organization, and the United Nations, which enables it to play an active role in regional cooperation and global affairs.

Demographics and languages spoken

Demographics

Fiji has a diverse population of around 900,000 people. The two largest ethnic groups are the indigenous Fijians (iTaukei), who make up approximately 56.8% of the population, and Indo-Fijians, who account for about 37.5%. The remaining population consists of smaller ethnic groups, such as Rotumans, Chinese, Europeans, and other Pacific Islanders.

Indigenous Fijians are predominantly of Melanesian and Polynesian ancestry, while the Indo-Fijian community is primarily descended from indentured labourers who were brought to Fiji from India by the British colonial government in the late 19th and early 20th centuries. The diversity of Fiji's population has contributed to the rich cultural tapestry of the country, but it has also been a source of tension and conflict in the past.

Languages Spoken

Fiji is a multilingual country with three official languages: English, Fijian (iTaukei), and Hindi.

English is the primary language used in government, business, and education. It is widely spoken and understood throughout the country, serving as a lingua franca between different ethnic groups. English was introduced during the British colonial period and has remained an important language in Fiji since gaining independence.

Fijian, also known as iTaukei or Bauan, is an Austronesian language spoken by the indigenous Fijian population. It is one of the more than 300 languages in the Oceanic subgroup of the Austronesian language family. Fijian is taught in schools and used in various aspects of daily life, such as traditional ceremonies, local media, and informal communication.

Hindi, specifically Fiji Hindi or Fiji Baat, is spoken by the Indo-Fijian community. Fiji Hindi is a distinct dialect that has evolved from several Indian languages, primarily Awadhi, Bhojpuri, and Standard Hindi, with influences from Fijian and English. It is used primarily in the home, religious institutions, and cultural events but is also taught in some schools.

In addition to the official languages, there are several other minority languages spoken by different ethnic communities in Fiji, such as Rotuman, Chinese dialects, and other Pacific Island languages.

3. CORE VALUES AND BELIEFS

Religion and Spirituality

Overview of Religious Landscape

Major religious affiliations in Fiji: Christianity, Hinduism, Islam, and indigenous belief systems

Fiji, a Melanesian archipelago in the South Pacific, is a diverse and multicultural nation, characterized by a rich tapestry of ethnicities, languages, and religions. The religious landscape in Fiji is primarily shaped by four major affiliations: Christianity, Hinduism, Islam, and indigenous belief systems. This diverse religious composition can be attributed to the nation's complex history, which includes colonization, indentured labour, and missionary work.

Christianity: Christianity is the dominant religion in Fiji, with a significant majority of the population identifying as Christian. This prominence can be traced back to the arrival of European missionaries, primarily from the Methodist Church, in the 19th century. These missionaries sought to convert the indigenous population, and their efforts were largely successful. Today, various denominations of Christianity, such as Methodism, Roman Catholicism, Seventh-day Adventism, and Assemblies of God, coexist in Fijian society.

Hinduism: The second largest religious group in Fiji is Hinduism, which is predominantly practiced by the Indo-Fijian community. Hinduism was introduced to Fiji in the late 19th and early 20th centuries by indentured labourers who were brought from India by the British colonial government to work on sugar plantations. The Hindu community in Fiji is diverse in terms of beliefs and practices, as it incorporates various traditions from different regions of India. Hinduism has played a significant role in shaping the cultural and religious identity of the Indo-Fijian population.

Islam: Islam is another religion practiced by a smaller percentage of the population in Fiji, mostly by the Indo-Fijian community. Like Hinduism, Islam was brought to Fiji by Indian indentured labourers during the British colonial period. The Muslim population in Fiji is diverse, as it includes followers of both the Sunni and Shia branches of Islam, as well as the smaller Ahmadiyya community. Islamic organizations and mosques in Fiji cater to the spiritual needs of the Muslim community and help preserve their cultural and religious heritage.

Indigenous belief systems: Prior to the arrival of Christianity, indigenous Fijians practiced their traditional belief systems, which involved a complex set of rituals, customs, and beliefs. These belief systems were closely tied to the natural world, ancestral spirits, and supernatural beings. Although the majority of indigenous Fijians have converted to Christianity, some elements of their traditional beliefs and practices continue to coexist and influence contemporary Fijian society. Indigenous ceremonies and rituals are still observed during important events such as births, weddings, and funerals.

Historical background and the influence of colonialism on religious practices

Fiji's historical background and the influence of colonialism have played a significant role in shaping the religious practices in Fijian society. Before the arrival of Europeans, indigenous Fijians followed their traditional belief systems, which were deeply rooted in their culture and way of life. These beliefs were closely tied to the natural world, ancestral spirits, and supernatural beings.

European contact and the arrival of Christianity: The first Europeans to arrive in Fiji were Dutch explorer Abel Tasman in 1643 and British navigator James Cook in 1774. However, it was not until the early 19th century that significant European contact began, primarily through the activities of traders, whalers, and sandalwood merchants. The arrival of Christian missionaries, predominantly from the Methodist Church, had a profound impact on the religious landscape of Fiji. They sought to convert the indigenous population, and their efforts were largely successful, leading to the widespread adoption of Christianity among Fijians. The influence of Christian missionaries led to the decline of traditional indigenous religious practices, although some elements of these practices have persisted and continue to coexist with Christianity.

British colonial rule and the introduction of other religions: Fiji became a British colony in 1874, which brought significant changes to the socio-political landscape of the country. One major change was the introduction of indentured laborers from India, who were brought to work on sugar plantations. These laborers, who arrived in Fiji between 1879 and 1916, practiced Hinduism and Islam. The arrival of these religions further diversified the religious landscape of Fiji and contributed to the development of a multicultural society.

Religious institutions during the colonial period: The British colonial administration sought to maintain social order and stability by recognizing and supporting various religious institutions. The Methodist Church, in particular, received significant support from the colonial administration, which enabled it to consolidate its influence and expand its activities in Fiji. This support contributed to the prominence of Christianity in Fijian society. At the same time, the colonial administration facilitated the establishment of Hindu and Muslim institutions, such as temples and mosques, to cater to the spiritual needs of the indentured labourers.

Post-independence and religious pluralism: Fiji gained independence from British colonial rule in 1970. In the years since independence, Fiji has experienced periods of political instability, including several military coups. Despite these challenges, the country has maintained a strong tradition of religious pluralism and tolerance. The constitution of Fiji recognizes the right to freedom of religion and guarantees the protection of religious practices for all citizens. This legal framework, along with the shared history of colonialism, has contributed to the harmonious coexistence of different religious communities in Fijian society.

Religious freedom and tolerance in Fiji

Religious freedom and tolerance are important aspects of Fijian society, as they contribute to the harmonious coexistence of diverse religious communities in the country. The religious landscape of Fiji, which includes Christianity, Hinduism, Islam, and indigenous belief systems, reflects the nation's multicultural history and complex colonial past. The concept of religious freedom and tolerance in Fiji can be understood through the following dimensions:

Constitutional provisions: The Fijian constitution recognizes the right to freedom of religion and guarantees the protection of religious practices for all citizens. This legal framework ensures that individuals have the right to practice their religion without interference from the state or other religious communities. The constitution also prohibits any form of religious discrimination, which promotes a culture of tolerance and respect for diverse religious beliefs.

Interfaith dialogue and cooperation: Fijian society has a strong tradition of interfaith dialogue and cooperation among different religious communities. Religious organizations, leaders, and individuals regularly engage in dialogue to promote understanding, tolerance, and peaceful coexistence. This includes participating in each other's religious celebrations and events, which fosters a sense of unity and solidarity among different faiths.

Religious education and awareness: In Fiji, religious education is incorporated into the public school curriculum, which provides students with a basic understanding of different religious traditions and promotes a culture of tolerance and respect for diverse beliefs. Additionally, religious organizations often engage in community outreach programs and educational initiatives to raise awareness about their respective faiths and foster understanding among different religious communities.

Government support for religious institutions: The Fijian government supports religious institutions by providing funding and resources for their activities, which helps maintain a balance among different faiths and contributes to religious tolerance. This support also ensures that religious organizations can cater to the spiritual needs of their respective communities without fear of persecution or discrimination.

Social acceptance and respect for diversity: Fijians are generally known for their warm hospitality and welcoming attitude towards people from different cultural and religious backgrounds. This social acceptance and respect for diversity contribute significantly to the overall atmosphere of religious tolerance in the country.

Christianity in Fiji

The introduction of Christianity through missionaries and its spread among the population

The introduction of Christianity through missionaries and its spread among the population in Fijian society is a significant historical event that has shaped the religious landscape of the country. The process can be understood through several key phases:

Early European contact: European explorers, such as Dutch explorer Abel Tasman and British navigator James Cook, contacted the Fijian archipelago in the 17th and 18th centuries. However, it was not until the early 19th century that sustained European contact began, primarily through the activities of traders, whalers, and sandalwood merchants.

Arrival of Christian missionaries: The first Christian missionaries arrived in Fiji in the early 19th century. These missionaries, predominantly from the Methodist Church, were motivated by the desire to convert the indigenous population to Christianity. They were followed by missionaries from other denominations, such as the Roman Catholic Church and the London Missionary Society. The missionaries used various strategies to spread Christianity, including establishing mission stations, schools, and medical facilities to serve the local population.

Conversion of Fijian chiefs and leaders: A crucial factor in the spread of Christianity among the indigenous Fijian population was the conversion of influential chiefs and leaders. These conversions often had a cascading effect, as the followers of these chiefs were more likely to adopt the new religion. One of the most notable examples is the conversion of Ratu Seru Cakobau, a powerful Fijian chief who declared himself a Christian in 1854 and played a significant role in the spread of Christianity in Fiji.

Role of Fijian teachers and preachers: Indigenous Fijians who had converted to Christianity also played an essential role in the spread of the religion. Many of them became teachers and preachers, helping to translate the Bible and other religious texts into the Fijian language, and providing religious education and guidance to their fellow Fijians. This localized approach to evangelization helped make Christianity more relatable and accessible to the indigenous population.

The decline of indigenous belief systems: The spread of Christianity in Fiji led to a decline in traditional indigenous belief systems, which were rooted in the worship of ancestral spirits and supernatural beings. The influence of Christian missionaries and the adoption of Christianity by indigenous Fijians led to the diminishing importance of these traditional beliefs, although some elements of these practices have persisted and continue to coexist with Christianity.

Consolidation of Christian denominations: Over time, various Christian denominations began to consolidate their presence in Fiji. The Methodist Church emerged as the largest and most influential denomination, followed by the Roman Catholic Church, the Seventh-day Adventist Church, and the Assemblies of God, among others. These denominations have established churches, schools, and other institutions to cater to the spiritual and educational needs of the Fijian population.

The role of Christianity in shaping Fijian culture and society

Christianity has played a significant role in shaping Fijian culture and society since its introduction in the 19th century. The adoption of Christianity by the indigenous Fijian population and its continued prominence have influenced various aspects of Fijian culture and society, including social norms, values, and practices. The following points describe and explain the role of Christianity in shaping Fijian culture and society:

Syncretism and the blending of cultural practices: The adoption of Christianity by indigenous Fijians led to a process of syncretism, wherein elements of traditional Fijian culture and belief systems were combined with Christian beliefs and practices. This blending of cultural practices can be seen in various aspects of Fijian society, such as rituals, ceremonies, and religious celebrations, where both Christian and traditional indigenous elements coexist.

Influence on social norms and values: Christianity has had a significant impact on the social norms and values of Fijian society. It introduced new moral and ethical principles, such as the importance of honesty, forgiveness, and compassion, which have become deeply ingrained in Fijian culture. Additionally, the influence of Christian missionaries led to the abolition of certain traditional practices, such as cannibalism, which were deemed incompatible with Christian values.

Role in education and literacy: Christian missionaries played a critical role in the development of education in Fiji by establishing mission schools, where indigenous Fijians were taught to read and write in their native language and English. This emphasis on education and literacy contributed to the development of a more educated population, which in turn influenced Fijian society's social and economic development.

Influence on artistic and cultural expression: Christianity has also shaped Fijian artistic and cultural expression, particularly in areas such as music, dance, and visual arts. For example, Fijian hymns and religious songs, often accompanied by traditional instruments, have become an integral part of Fijian culture. Likewise, religious themes and symbols are frequently incorporated into Fijian art and handicrafts.

Impact on family and community structure: The adoption of Christianity has influenced the family and community structure in Fijian society. Christian values, such as the sanctity of marriage and the importance of family unity, have reinforced traditional Fijian customs related to family life and social organization. Furthermore, the church has become an essential institution in Fijian society, serving as a centre for community gatherings, celebrations, and social support.

Promotion of social cohesion and unity: Christianity has played a role in promoting social cohesion and unity among the diverse ethnic and cultural groups in Fiji. The shared experience of conversion to Christianity and participation in religious practices and celebrations has contributed to a sense of shared identity among indigenous Fijians, which has been essential in fostering social harmony in the country.

Main denominations: Methodist, Roman Catholic, Seventh-day Adventist, and Assemblies of God

In Fijian society, Christianity is the dominant religion, and it is divided into several main denominations, including the Methodist Church, the Roman Catholic Church, the Seventh-day Adventist Church, and the Assemblies of God. These denominations coexist and play significant roles in shaping Fijian culture and society in various ways:

Methodist Church: The Methodist Church is the largest and most influential Christian denomination in Fiji, with roots tracing back to the early 19th century when the first Methodist missionaries arrived in the country. The Methodist Church has had a significant impact on Fijian society by promoting education, healthcare, and social services through the establishment of schools, hospitals, and community centres. The church has also played a vital role in promoting social cohesion and unity among indigenous Fijians, fostering a sense of shared identity, and belonging.

Roman Catholic Church: The Roman Catholic Church is the second-largest Christian denomination in Fiji, with a history dating back to the mid-19th century when French Marist missionaries first arrived. The Roman Catholic Church has contributed to Fijian society through its extensive network of schools, hospitals, and social services. The church has also promoted interfaith dialogue and cooperation, working with other religious communities to foster understanding and tolerance in Fiji.

Seventh-day Adventist Church: The Seventh-day Adventist Church is another significant Christian denomination in Fiji, which was introduced in the late 19th century. The church emphasizes the importance of holistic health and wellbeing, operating several schools, hospitals, and health centres in the country. The Seventh-day Adventist Church also promotes a distinct set of beliefs, such as observing the Sabbath on Saturday, which has contributed to the religious diversity in Fijian society.

Assemblies of God: The Assemblies of God is a Pentecostal Christian denomination that was introduced to Fiji in the early 20th century. The church is known for its emphasis on the spiritual gifts of the Holy Spirit, such as speaking in tongues, prophecy, and divine healing. The Assemblies of God has contributed to Fijian society through its network of churches and community outreach programs, as well as its focus on spiritual revival and personal transformation.

Each of these Christian denominations has influenced Fijian culture and society in distinct ways, while also sharing certain commonalities. They have all played crucial roles in providing education, healthcare, and social services, which have contributed to the development and wellbeing of Fijian communities. Additionally, these denominations have all been active in promoting social cohesion, unity, and religious tolerance, fostering a culture of understanding and respect for diverse beliefs in Fijian society.

Furthermore, these denominations have shaped Fijian culture and society through their influence on moral and ethical values, artistic and cultural expression, family and community structures, and social norms. As a result, the Methodist Church, the Roman Catholic Church, the Seventh-day Adventist

Church, and the Assemblies of God have all left lasting impacts on Fijian culture and society, reflecting the rich and diverse religious landscape of the country.

Hinduism in Fiji

The arrival of Hinduism with the indentured labourers from India

The arrival of Hinduism with the indentured labourers from India has had a significant impact on Fijian culture and society. The introduction of this new religion and its subsequent influence can be understood through several key stages and factors:

Indentured labour system and the arrival of Indians: From 1879 to 1916, the British colonial administration in Fiji brought thousands of indentured labourers from India to work on sugar plantations. These labourers, who were primarily from northern and southern India, practiced Hinduism, as well as Islam and other religious traditions.

Introduction of Hinduism: The arrival of indentured labourers marked the beginning of the Hindu presence in Fiji. Hinduism, with its diverse beliefs, practices, and rituals, added to the religious landscape of Fiji, enriching its multicultural society. The Indian labourers built temples and shrines, maintained their religious practices, and celebrated Hindu festivals, despite the challenges of living in a foreign land under difficult circumstances.

Preservation of Indian culture and traditions: The indentured labourers and their descendants made efforts to preserve their cultural and religious traditions, including the practice of Hinduism, in the face of an unfamiliar environment and the dominance of Christianity. They established religious and cultural organizations, as well as schools, to teach the younger generation about their heritage, language, and traditions. This determination to preserve their culture and religious practices has contributed to the resilience and vibrancy of the Indian Fijian community.

Impact on Fijian society: The introduction of Hinduism and the presence of the Indian Fijian community have had a lasting impact on Fijian society. The religious diversity brought by Hinduism has fostered a more inclusive and tolerant society. Fijians have come to appreciate the unique customs, rituals, and festivals of the Hindu community, which have become an integral part of the country's cultural landscape. Additionally, the Indian Fijian community has made significant contributions to Fiji's economy, politics, and social development.

Interfaith dialogue and cooperation: The coexistence of Hinduism with other religious traditions in Fiji, such as Christianity, Islam, and indigenous belief systems, has fostered interfaith dialogue and cooperation. Religious organizations, leaders, and individuals from different faiths often engage in dialogue and participate in each other's religious celebrations to promote understanding and tolerance.

Key beliefs, rituals, and festivals in the Fijian Hindu community

The Fijian Hindu community, which has its roots in the arrival of indentured labourers from India in the late 19th and early 20th centuries, has a rich and diverse religious tradition. Key beliefs, rituals, and festivals in the Fijian Hindu community can be explained through the following aspects:

Key beliefs: Fijian Hindus follow the broader principles of Hinduism, which include the belief in a Supreme Being (Brahman), the concept of dharma (duty or righteousness), karma (the law of cause and effect), and the cycle of birth, death, and rebirth (samsara). Fijian Hindus also worship a multitude of gods and goddesses, such as Shiva, Vishnu, and Durga, who are seen as manifestations of the Supreme Being.

Rituals: The Fijian Hindu community follows a variety of rituals that are integral to their religious practice. These rituals can be divided into daily, periodic, and occasional rituals. Daily rituals include prayer (puja) and meditation, often performed in front of a home shrine. Periodic rituals include fasting and observing specific days dedicated to particular deities, such as Shivratri (dedicated to Lord Shiva) or Ekadashi (dedicated to Lord Vishnu). Occasional rituals include rites of passage, such as birth, marriage, and death ceremonies, which involve various religious and cultural customs.

Festivals: The Fijian Hindu community celebrates several festivals throughout the year, which are marked by religious ceremonies, cultural performances, and social gatherings. Some key festivals include:

a. Diwali: Also known as the Festival of Lights, Diwali is one of the most significant Hindu festivals celebrated by the Fijian Hindu community. It marks the victory of light over darkness and good over evil. The festival involves the lighting of oil lamps, fireworks, feasting, and the exchange of gifts and sweets.

b. Holi: The festival of colours, Holi, is another prominent Hindu festival celebrated by Fijian Hindus. The festival signifies the triumph of good over evil and the arrival of spring. It is characterized by the throwing of coloured powder and water, singing, dancing, and feasting.

c. Navratri: Navratri is a nine-night festival dedicated to the worship of the goddess Durga and her various forms. It is marked by religious observances, fasting, prayers, and cultural performances, such as the traditional Indian dance called Garba.

d. Ram Navami: This festival celebrates the birth of Lord Rama, one of the most important incarnations of the god Vishnu. Ram Navami is observed with prayer, fasting, and the recitation of the Ramayana, an ancient Indian epic that narrates the life of Lord Rama.

e. Krishna Janmashtami: The festival commemorates the birth of Lord Krishna, another significant incarnation of the god Vishnu. Celebrations involve fasting, prayer, devotional singing, and the enactment of scenes from Lord Krishna's life.

The influence of Hinduism on Fijian culture and the lives of Indo-Fijians

Hinduism, introduced to Fiji by indentured labourers from India, has had a significant influence on Fijian culture and the lives of Indo-Fijians. The impact of Hinduism can be seen in various aspects of Fijian society, including religious practices, cultural expressions, and social norms. The following points describe and explain the influence of Hinduism on Fijian culture and the lives of Indo-Fijians:

Religious practices: The practice of Hinduism has shaped the religious landscape of Fiji by adding to its religious diversity. Hindu temples and shrines can be found across the country, serving as centres for worship, education, and community gatherings. Additionally, Hindu rituals and customs, such as prayer, fasting, and festivals, have become an integral part of the religious experience for Indo-Fijians.

Cultural expressions: Hinduism has influenced Fijian culture through various forms of artistic and cultural expression, including music, dance, and visual arts. Indian classical music and dance forms, such as Kathak, Bharatanatyam, and Odissi, have been adapted and incorporated into Fijian culture. Moreover, traditional Indian crafts, such as textile weaving, pottery, and jewellery making, have been integrated into Fijian handicrafts, enriching the country's artistic heritage.

Language and literature: Hinduism's impact on Fijian culture can also be seen in language and literature. Hindi, the primary language of many Indo-Fijians, has influenced Fijian vocabulary and linguistic expressions. Furthermore, Hindu religious texts, such as the Bhagavad Gita, Ramayana, and Mahabharata, have been translated into Fijian languages, contributing to the country's literary heritage.

Festivals and celebrations: Hindu festivals, such as Diwali, Holi, and Navratri, have become an integral part of Fijian culture. These celebrations, marked by colourful processions, traditional music, and dance performances, contribute to the multicultural character of Fiji, and promote interfaith understanding and cooperation.

Social norms and values: Hinduism has shaped the social norms and values of Indo-Fijians, influencing family structure, marriage customs, and social etiquette. Traditional Hindu values, such as respect for elders, the importance of family, and the observance of religious rituals, continue to play a significant role in the lives of Indo-Fijians.

Cuisine: The influence of Hinduism is also evident in Fijian cuisine as Indian culinary traditions have been integrated into Fijian food culture. Dishes such as curry, roti, and various vegetarian options have become popular in Fiji, reflecting the dietary restrictions and preferences of the Hindu community.

Interfaith dialogue and cooperation: The presence of Hinduism in Fiji has contributed to the development of interfaith dialogue and cooperation among different religious communities. This has fostered an environment of religious tolerance and understanding, as people from diverse faiths come together to appreciate and learn from each other's customs and traditions.

Islam in Fiji

The introduction of Islam with the arrival of Muslim indentured laborers from India

The introduction of Islam in Fijian society can be traced back to the arrival of Muslim indentured laborers from India in the late 19th and early 20th centuries. This new religious tradition has had a lasting impact on Fijian culture and society in various ways:

Arrival of Muslim indentured labourers: Between 1879 and 1916, the British colonial administration brought thousands of indentured labourers from India to work on sugar plantations in Fiji. Among these labourers were Muslims, who came primarily from the regions of Uttar Pradesh, Bihar, and Gujarat. They brought with them their religious beliefs, customs, and practices.

Introduction of Islam: The Muslim indentured labourers introduced Islam to Fiji, adding to the country's religious diversity. They established mosques and madrasas (Islamic religious schools) to preserve and practice their faith. The Fijian Muslim community initially comprised mainly of Sunni Muslims, following the Hanafi school of Islamic jurisprudence.

Preservation of Islamic culture and traditions: Despite facing challenges in a foreign land and a predominantly Christian environment, the Muslim labourers and their descendants made efforts to preserve their Islamic culture and religious traditions. They formed organizations and institutions to support their community, provide religious education, and ensure the continuation of their cultural and religious practices.

Impact on Fijian society: The introduction of Islam and the presence of the Muslim community have had a lasting impact on Fijian society. The religious diversity brought by Islam has fostered a more inclusive and tolerant society. Fijians have come to appreciate the unique customs, rituals, and celebrations of the Muslim community, which have become an integral part of Fiji's multicultural landscape.

Contributions to Fiji's development: The Muslim community in Fiji has made significant contributions to the country's development in various fields, such as trade, business, politics, and social services. They have also been instrumental in promoting education, establishing schools, and contributing to the overall wellbeing of Fijian society.

Interfaith dialogue and cooperation: The coexistence of Islam with other religious traditions in Fiji, such as Christianity, Hinduism, and indigenous belief systems, has fostered interfaith dialogue and cooperation. Religious organizations, leaders, and individuals from different faiths often engage in dialogue and participate in each other's religious celebrations to promote understanding and tolerance.

The Sunni and Ahmadiyya Muslim communities in Fiji

In Fiji, the Muslim community is primarily composed of two sects: Sunni and Ahmadiyya. Both communities have their distinct beliefs, practices, and histories, contributing to the religious diversity in Fijian society.

Sunni Muslim Community: Sunni Muslims form the majority of the Muslim population in Fiji. They mainly follow the Hanafi school of Islamic jurisprudence, which is one of the four major Sunni schools of thought.

    a. Origins: The Sunni Muslim community in Fiji traces its roots back to the arrival of Muslim indentured labourers from India during the British colonial era (1879-1916). These labourers were primarily from the regions of Uttar Pradesh, Bihar, and Gujarat.

    b. Religious practices: The Sunni Muslims in Fiji adhere to traditional Islamic practices, such as observing the five daily prayers, fasting during the month of Ramadan, giving alms (zakat), and performing the Hajj pilgrimage to Mecca when financially and physically able.

    c. Institutions and organizations: Sunni Muslims in Fiji have established mosques, madrasas (Islamic religious schools), and community organizations to cater to their religious and cultural needs. The Fiji Muslim League is one of the prominent organizations representing the interests of the Sunni Muslim community and providing essential services such as education, healthcare, and social welfare.

    d. Cultural integration: Sunni Muslims in Fiji have integrated into Fijian society while maintaining their cultural and religious identity. They have contributed to the country's development in various fields and have actively participated in interfaith dialogue and cooperation.

Ahmadiyya Muslim Community

The Ahmadiyya Muslim community is a smaller sect within Islam that originated in the late 19th century in Qadian, India. Their presence in Fiji is relatively more recent compared to the Sunni Muslim community.

    a. Origins: The Ahmadiyya Muslim community in Fiji was established in the 1960s when Ahmadiyya missionaries arrived from Pakistan and India. They began spreading their message and converting local Sunni Muslims and other Fijians to their interpretation of Islam.

    b. Beliefs and practices: The Ahmadiyya community differs from mainstream Sunni Islam in some key theological respects, particularly concerning the status of their founder, Mirza Ghulam Ahmad. Ahmadis believe that Mirza Ghulam Ahmad was the Promised Messiah and Mahdi awaited by Muslims, while Sunni Muslims reject this claim. Despite these differences, Ahmadi Muslims follow similar Islamic practices, such as daily prayers, fasting, and charity.

    c. Institutions and organizations: The Ahmadiyya Muslim community in Fiji has established its mosques and community centres to serve their religious needs. They also have their organizations, such as the Ahmadiyya Muslim Jama'at Fiji, which is responsible for managing their community affairs and promoting their religious teachings.

d. Challenges and acceptance: The Ahmadiyya community has faced challenges in Fiji, including occasional tensions with the Sunni Muslim community due to theological differences. However, they have continued to practice their faith and engage in interfaith dialogue and cooperation.

Religious practices and the influence of Islam on the Fijian Muslim community

Religious practices and the influence of Islam on the Fijian Muslim community can be seen in various aspects of their lives, including religious observances, cultural expressions, social norms, and interfaith relations. Here is an overview of these aspects:

Religious observances: Fijian Muslims adhere to the fundamental tenets and practices of Islam. Some key observances include:

a. **The Five Pillars of Islam**: Fijian Muslims follow the Five Pillars, which are the core principles and practices of Islam. These include Shahada (declaration of faith), Salah (daily prayers), Zakat (almsgiving), Sawm (fasting during Ramadan), and Hajj (pilgrimage to Mecca).
b. **Prayer**: Fijian Muslims perform the five daily prayers (Fajr, Dhuhr, Asr, Maghrib, and Isha) and attend congregational prayers at mosques, especially on Fridays for Jumu'ah prayer.
c. **Ramadan and Eid al-Fitr**: Fijian Muslims observe the holy month of Ramadan by fasting from dawn to sunset and engaging in increased prayer and spiritual reflection. The end of Ramadan is marked by the celebration of Eid al-Fitr, a festival characterized by communal prayers, feasting, and giving to the less fortunate.
d. **Eid al-Adha**: This festival commemorates the willingness of Prophet Ibrahim (Abraham) to sacrifice his son in obedience to God's command. Fijian Muslims celebrate Eid al-Adha with special prayers, the sacrifice of an animal (such as a goat or sheep), and the distribution of meat to family, friends, and the needy.

Cultural expressions have influenced Fijian culture in various ways

a. **Clothing**: Fijian Muslims often wear modest clothing in adherence to Islamic principles. Men may wear traditional attire like the kurta (long tunic) and women may wear the hijab (headscarf) and abaya (loose-fitting robe).
b. **Language**: Arabic, the language of the Quran, is used in religious contexts and Islamic education, while the majority of Fijian Muslims speak English and Fiji Hindi in daily life.
c. **Arts**: Islamic art, such as calligraphy and geometric patterns, can be found in mosques and religious artefacts in the Fijian Muslim community.
d. **Social norms and values**: Islamic teachings have shaped the social norms and values of Fijian Muslims, influencing areas like family structure, marriage customs, and gender roles. Traditional Islamic values, such as respect for elders, modesty, and the importance of community, continue to play a significant role in the lives of Fijian Muslims.
e. **Interfaith dialogue and cooperation**: The presence of Islam in Fiji has contributed to the development of interfaith dialogue and cooperation among different religious communities.

This has fostered a more inclusive and tolerant society, as people from diverse faiths come together to appreciate and learn from each other's customs and traditions.

Indigenous Fijian Spirituality

Traditional Fijian beliefs and practices before the arrival of Christianity

Before the arrival of Christianity, Fijian society was characterized by a complex system of traditional beliefs and practices rooted in animism, ancestral worship, and polytheism. These beliefs and practices played a crucial role in shaping the social, cultural, and political life of pre-Christian Fijian society. Some key aspects of traditional Fijian beliefs and practices include:

Animism: Fijians believed that natural objects, elements, and phenomena possessed spirits or supernatural powers. This animistic worldview led to the veneration of various natural elements such as the sun, the moon, the sea, and the land. Fijians believed that maintaining harmony with these spirits was essential for the well-being and prosperity of their communities.

Ancestral worship: Ancestral spirits played a central role in traditional Fijian religion. Fijians believed that the spirits of their ancestors could influence the world of the living, providing protection, guidance, and blessings. They sought to maintain a connection with their ancestors through rituals, offerings, and the preservation of ancestral relics.

Polytheism: Fijian society was marked by the worship of numerous gods and deities. These gods were associated with various aspects of life, such as agriculture, war, and fertility. The most widely venerated gods included Degei, the supreme god and creator, and Ravuyalo, the god of the underworld.

Social hierarchy and religious roles: Traditional Fijian society was highly hierarchical, with a well-defined social structure. The high chiefs (Ratu) held both political and religious power and were considered semi-divine. Beneath the chiefs were the priests (Bete), who played a crucial role in communicating with the gods and ancestral spirits. They presided over religious rituals and ceremonies, ensuring the maintenance of spiritual balance and harmony within the community.

Rituals and ceremonies: Fijian religious life was marked by numerous rituals and ceremonies intended to maintain harmony with the spiritual world. These rituals included offerings of food, kava (a traditional drink made from the roots of the kava plant), and other valuables to the gods and ancestral spirits. Ceremonies also marked significant life events such as births, marriages, and deaths, as well as communal events like the construction of a new temple or the launch of a war canoe.

Taboo system (tabu): Traditional Fijian society had a complex system of taboos that governed social behaviour and interactions. Taboos were based on the belief that certain actions, objects, or places possessed sacred or dangerous powers that could bring misfortune if not respected. The violation of taboos could result in severe consequences, including illness, crop failure, or even death.

Cannibalism: Although not a widespread practice, cannibalism was present in some parts of pre-Christian Fijian society. It was often associated with warfare and was believed to demonstrate power, instil fear, and appease the gods.

The concept of "vanua" (land) and its spiritual significance

The concept of "vanua" holds deep cultural and spiritual significance in Fijian society. It refers to the land, but also encompasses a broader understanding that includes the people, their culture, history, and their relationship with the environment. Vanua is an integral part of Fijian identity and is rooted in the following aspects:

Connection to ancestors: Fijians believe that their ancestors' spirits are intertwined with the land, and they consider the vanua as their ancestral home. The land is a living embodiment of their forebears, and Fijians maintain a strong connection to their ancestors by respecting and protecting the vanua.

Social structure and identity: The vanua is the foundation of Fijian social structure and identity. Fijian society is organized into clans (mataqali) and sub-clans (tokatoka), which are connected to specific territories. Each clan has a unique history, customs, and traditions associated with their land, contributing to their sense of belonging and identity.

Spiritual significance: Fijians view the vanua as a sacred space imbued with spiritual power. They believe that gods, ancestral spirits, and other supernatural beings reside in or are associated with specific places within the vanua, such as mountains, forests, rivers, and the sea. As such, the land is deeply intertwined with the spiritual well-being of the community.

Stewardship and environmental conservation: The concept of vanua emphasizes the importance of taking care of the land and its resources. Fijians believe that they are stewards of the vanua, responsible for maintaining harmony with the environment and ensuring its sustainability for future generations. This is reflected in traditional practices such as sustainable farming, fishing, and resource management.

Reciprocal relationship: Fijians believe in a reciprocal relationship between the people and the vanua. The land provides sustenance, protection, and a sense of identity, while the people, in turn, must respect, protect, and preserve the land to ensure the continued wellbeing of the community.

Land rights and ownership: Landownership in Fiji is predominantly communal, with the vanua being held collectively by the indigenous Fijian people. This communal ownership is an essential aspect of Fijian culture and reflects the interconnectedness of the people with the land and their environment.

The role of ancestral spirits and traditional rituals in Fijian culture

Ancestral spirits and traditional rituals play a significant role in Fijian culture, shaping the social, spiritual, and cultural aspects of life. These elements have been essential in maintaining the connection between the living and the spiritual world and ensuring the well-being and harmony of Fijian communities.

Ancestral spirits: In traditional Fijian beliefs, ancestral spirits, known as "kalou vu," hold great importance. Fijians believe that these spirits continue to influence the living world by providing guidance, protection, and blessings. Ancestral spirits are often associated with specific places, such as burial grounds, sacred sites, or natural landmarks. It is believed that maintaining a strong connection with these spirits is vital for the welfare and prosperity of the community.

Traditional rituals: Various traditional rituals and ceremonies have been developed to honour and maintain connections with ancestral spirits, as well as to ensure harmony between the living and the spiritual world. These rituals include:

a. **Offerings and sacrifices**: Fijians offer food, kava, and other valuable items to ancestral spirits as a sign of respect and gratitude. In some instances, animal sacrifices were performed to appease the spirits or to seek their favour during critical events such as warfare, drought, or illness.

b. **Spirit houses (bure kalou)**: In traditional Fijian villages, spirit houses were constructed to serve as sacred spaces where rituals and ceremonies could be performed to communicate with ancestral spirits. These structures were often adorned with intricate carvings and designs representing the spirits and their powers.

c. **Life-cycle rituals**: Traditional Fijian rituals mark significant life events, such as birth, puberty, marriage, and death. These ceremonies often involve offerings and prayers to ancestral spirits, seeking their blessings and protection during these critical transitions.

d. **Community rituals and ceremonies**: Fijian communities engage in various rituals and ceremonies to ensure the harmony and well-being of the community as a whole. These may include rituals for successful harvests, the construction of a new temple or war canoe, or the appointment of a new chief.

e. **Social cohesion and cultural identity**: Ancestral spirits and traditional rituals play a vital role in reinforcing social cohesion and cultural identity among Fijians. Participation in these rituals helps to strengthen bonds within the community, pass on cultural knowledge and traditions to younger generations, and maintain a sense of belonging and continuity.

f. **Adaptation and change**: With the arrival of Christianity and other external influences, some aspects of Fijian ancestral beliefs and traditional rituals have changed or diminished. However, many Fijians still incorporate elements of their traditional spirituality into their lives, and certain rituals and practices have been adapted to coexist with Christian beliefs.

Syncretism and Interfaith Dialogue

The blending of traditional Fijian beliefs with Christianity, Hinduism, and Islam

The blending of traditional Fijian beliefs with Christianity, Hinduism, and Islam has resulted in a unique and diverse religious landscape in Fiji. This syncretism is a testament to the adaptability and resilience of Fijian culture, which has embraced elements of different faiths while maintaining a connection to its ancestral roots. Here is an overview of how traditional Fijian beliefs have blended with these major religions:

<u>Christianity</u>: Christianity was introduced to Fiji in the 19th century by European missionaries, and it has since become the dominant religion among the indigenous Fijian population. While many traditional Fijian beliefs and practices have changed or faded away due to the influence of Christianity, some aspects of Fijian spirituality have been incorporated into the new faith. For example:

   a. **Ancestral spirits and saints**: Some Fijians have found parallels between their ancestral spirits and Christian saints, venerating them as intercessors between the human and divine realms.
   b. **Rituals and ceremonies**: Traditional Fijian rituals and ceremonies have been adapted to fit within a Christian context, such as the use of kava during church gatherings or the incorporation of Fijian chants and music in Christian worship.
   c. **Sacred spaces**: Some Fijians continue to revere traditional sacred sites alongside Christian places of worship, acknowledging the spiritual power associated with these locations.

<u>Hinduism</u>: Hinduism was introduced to Fiji by indentured labourers from India in the late 19th century, and it has become the primary religion among the Indo-Fijian population. The blending of Fijian and Hindu beliefs has resulted in a unique form of Hinduism that incorporates local traditions and practices. For instance:

   a. Deities and spirits: Some Fijian Hindus have incorporated elements of traditional Fijian beliefs into their worship, such as recognizing local spirits or adapting traditional myths and legends to fit within the Hindu pantheon.
   b. Festivals and celebrations: Fijian Hindus have adapted traditional Fijian customs and practices to celebrate Hindu festivals, such as incorporating Fijian music and dance into their celebrations.

<u>Islam</u>: Islam was introduced to Fiji by Muslim indentured labourers from India, and it has since become a significant minority religion among the Indo-Fijian population. Although Islam has a more rigid theological structure than Christianity and Hinduism, there have still been instances of blending with Fijian beliefs and practices. Examples include:

a. Cultural expressions: Fijian Muslims have incorporated elements of Fijian culture into their religious practices, such as wearing traditional Fijian attire or using Fijian-language greetings and expressions in daily life.

b. Interfaith cooperation: Fijian Muslims, like their Hindu and Christian counterparts, have engaged in interfaith dialogue and cooperation, which has fostered mutual understanding and appreciation for each other's customs and traditions.

Examples of syncretism in religious practices and rituals

Syncretism in religious practices and rituals in Fiji is evident in the ways different religious traditions have adapted and incorporated elements from traditional Fijian beliefs and customs. Here are some examples of syncretism in Fijian religious practices:

Christian syncretism

a. Kava ceremonies: Kava, a traditional Fijian drink made from the roots of the kava plant, plays an essential role in various social and cultural gatherings. In Christian communities, kava ceremonies have been integrated into religious events, such as church gatherings, feasts, and celebrations.

b. Fijian hymns and music: Traditional Fijian music, chants, and instruments have been incorporated into Christian worship services, creating a unique blend of local and Christian musical expressions. Fijian hymns often feature Christian themes and biblical stories alongside references to Fijian culture and traditions.

c. Lotu (prayer) service: Some Fijian Christian communities hold traditional lotu services, where people gather to pray, sing hymns, and share kava. These services blend Fijian customs with Christian prayer and devotion.

Hindu syncretism

a. Deities and spirits: Some Fijian Hindus recognize local spirits and ancestral spirits within their religious practices. They might adapt traditional Fijian myths and legends to fit within the Hindu pantheon, creating a unique blend of local and Hindu beliefs.

b. Festivals and celebrations: Fijian Hindus celebrate traditional Hindu festivals with a Fijian touch, incorporating local music, dance, and customs into their festivities. For example, during Diwali, the festival of lights, Fijian Hindus might use traditional Fijian oil lamps alongside more conventional Indian oil lamps or candles.

Islamic syncretism

a. Cultural expressions: Fijian Muslims have integrated elements of Fijian culture into their religious practices. They might wear traditional Fijian attire, such as the sulu (a wraparound skirt), during prayers or religious gatherings, and use Fijian-language greetings and expressions in daily life.

b. Interfaith cooperation: Fijian Muslims, like their Hindu and Christian counterparts, engage in interfaith dialogue and cooperation. This interaction has fostered mutual understanding and appreciation for each other's customs and traditions, leading to occasional blending of religious practices during shared community events or celebrations.

The importance of interfaith dialogue and cooperation in fostering religious harmony in Fiji

Interfaith dialogue and cooperation play a crucial role in fostering religious harmony in Fiji, a country with a diverse religious landscape that includes Christianity, Hinduism, Islam, and traditional indigenous beliefs. By promoting understanding, respect, and tolerance among different religious communities, interfaith initiatives contribute to the social cohesion and stability of the nation. The importance of interfaith dialogue and cooperation in fostering religious harmony in Fiji can be understood through the following aspects:

Mutual understanding: Interfaith dialogue provides a platform for individuals and communities from different religious backgrounds to share their beliefs, values, and practices. This exchange of ideas promotes mutual understanding and appreciation, helping to break down barriers, dispel misconceptions, and reduce prejudices that may exist among religious groups.

Respect for diversity: By engaging in interfaith dialogue and cooperation, religious communities in Fiji can learn to appreciate and respect the diversity of beliefs and practices that exist within the nation. This respect for diversity is essential for fostering an inclusive and harmonious society, where individuals can freely practice their faith without fear of discrimination or persecution.

Conflict resolution and peacebuilding: Religious differences can sometimes lead to tensions and conflicts within communities. Interfaith dialogue and cooperation can serve as a tool for conflict resolution and peacebuilding by encouraging open communication, understanding, and empathy among different religious groups. By working together to address shared concerns and promote common values, religious communities can foster a sense of unity and harmony.

Social cohesion and collaboration: Interfaith initiatives often involve collaboration on social and community projects, such as providing support to vulnerable populations, addressing environmental issues, or promoting education and healthcare. By working together on these projects, religious communities can strengthen social bonds and foster a sense of shared responsibility for the well-being of the nation.

Preservation of cultural heritage: Interfaith dialogue and cooperation can also contribute to the preservation of Fiji's rich cultural heritage by promoting understanding and appreciation of the diverse religious traditions that have shaped the nation's history and identity. By engaging in interfaith initiatives, religious communities can learn from one another and preserve the unique aspects of their traditions while fostering a sense of national unity.

Religion and Public Life

The role of religion in Fijian politics and public life

Religion plays a significant role in Fijian politics and public life, shaping the social, cultural, and political landscape of the nation. While Fiji is constitutionally a secular state, religious beliefs and institutions have influenced various aspects of its political and public sphere. The role of religion in Fijian politics and public life can be explained through the following aspects:

Religious demographics: The religious composition of Fiji includes a majority of Christians, primarily among indigenous Fijians, and significant Hindu and Muslim populations, mainly among Indo-Fijians. This religious diversity has contributed to shaping the political landscape, as political parties often appeal to specific religious or ethnic constituencies to garner support.

Influence on political parties: Some political parties in Fiji have been historically associated with specific religious or ethnic groups. For instance, the Methodist Church has had a strong influence on indigenous Fijian politics and has been linked to the Fijian political party (SODELPA). Conversely, the National Federation Party (NFP) has traditionally represented the interests of the Indo-Fijian Hindu community. These connections between religious communities and political parties can impact political alliances, policies, and electoral outcomes.

Role of religious institutions and leaders: Religious institutions and leaders often play a prominent role in Fijian public life, providing guidance, moral authority, and support to their communities. They may also participate in public debates and discussions on various social, political, and ethical issues, influencing public opinion and policymaking. For example, religious leaders may advocate for or against specific policies based on their religious beliefs, such as promoting religious education in schools, addressing poverty and inequality, or advocating for environmental conservation.

Religion in public ceremonies and events: Religious rituals, prayers, and ceremonies are often incorporated into Fijian public life, including political events and state functions. This inclusion of religious elements in public ceremonies reflects the importance of religion in Fijian culture and its role in fostering national unity and identity.

Social issues and policy debates: Religion can also play a role in shaping public opinion and policy debates on various social issues, such as gender equality, LGBTQ+ rights, family planning, and education. Religious beliefs and values can inform the perspectives and positions of politicians, policymakers, and citizens on these matters, impacting the development and implementation of policies.

Interfaith dialogue in politics: The promotion of interfaith dialogue and cooperation among religious communities can contribute to fostering a sense of national unity and social cohesion in Fiji. By engaging in interfaith initiatives, political leaders can demonstrate their commitment to religious tolerance, pluralism, and inclusivity, which are essential for maintaining peace and stability in a diverse society.

The influence of religious organizations on social issues and development

Religious organizations play a vital role in addressing social issues and promoting development in many societies, including Fiji. They often engage in various activities, such as education, healthcare, poverty alleviation, and humanitarian assistance, contributing to the well-being of their communities. The influence of religious organizations on social issues and development can be described and explained through the following aspects:

Education: Many religious organizations operate schools, colleges, and other educational institutions, providing essential educational services to their communities. In Fiji, for example, Christian, Hindu, and Islamic organizations run schools that serve diverse populations. These institutions often promote their religious values and teachings alongside secular subjects, contributing to the moral and ethical development of their students.

Healthcare: Religious organizations are also involved in the provision of healthcare services, such as running hospitals, clinics, and other medical facilities. They may provide affordable or free healthcare services to vulnerable or marginalized populations, ensuring access to essential healthcare for those in need. In some cases, religious organizations also play a role in promoting public health initiatives and awareness campaigns on various health issues.

Poverty alleviation and social welfare: Religious organizations often engage in charitable activities aimed at alleviating poverty and addressing social welfare needs within their communities. They may offer food, clothing, shelter, and other forms of assistance to those in need, helping to alleviate suffering and improve living conditions. Moreover, religious organizations may also implement development projects that focus on income generation, skills development, and other forms of empowerment for disadvantaged groups.

Disaster relief and humanitarian assistance: In times of natural disasters or humanitarian crises, religious organizations often mobilize resources and volunteers to provide relief and assistance to affected populations. They may offer shelter, food, medical care, and other forms of support to those in need, working alongside other aid agencies and local governments to respond to emergencies.

Advocacy and social justice: Religious organizations can also play a role in advocating for social justice and human rights, addressing issues such as inequality, discrimination, and marginalization. They may raise awareness of these issues, lobby for policy changes, and promote initiatives aimed at fostering social inclusion and equality.

Environmental conservation: Some religious organizations are involved in environmental conservation efforts, recognizing the importance of protecting the natural world as part of their spiritual beliefs and values. They may engage in activities such as tree planting, waste management, and promotion of sustainable practices, contributing to the preservation and restoration of the environment.

Community building and social cohesion: Religious organizations often serve as important centres of community life, providing a space for people to gather, socialize, and support one another. By fostering a sense of belonging and shared identity, religious organizations can contribute to social cohesion and harmony within diverse societies.

The relationship between religious institutions and the government

The relationship between religious institutions and the Fijian government is shaped by the country's constitution, which guarantees freedom of religion and separation of church and state. This ensures that religious institutions can function independently of the government, and people can freely practice their faith without interference. However, religious institutions and the Fijian government still interact and collaborate in various ways to address social, cultural, and political issues. The relationship between them can be described and explained through the following aspects:

Constitutional framework: The Fijian Constitution guarantees freedom of religion and the right to worship, ensuring that religious institutions can operate without government interference. The constitution also emphasizes the secular nature of the state, ensuring that no single religion is given preference or established as the official religion of the country.

Collaboration on social issues and development: Religious institutions and the Fijian government often collaborate on social issues and development initiatives, such as education, healthcare, poverty alleviation, and disaster relief. Religious institutions may receive government support, including financial assistance and access to resources, to help implement various projects and programs that benefit society. In return, the government benefits from the expertise, reach, and resources of religious institutions in addressing social needs and challenges.

Interfaith dialogue and harmony: Both the Fijian government and religious institutions have a shared interest in promoting interfaith dialogue and religious harmony, recognizing the importance of tolerance and unity in a diverse society. The government may engage religious leaders and institutions in initiatives aimed at fostering understanding, respect, and cooperation among different faith communities, helping to maintain social cohesion and prevent religious conflict.

Influence on public policy: While the Fijian government is constitutionally secular, religious institutions can still influence public policy and political discourse through their involvement in social, cultural, and ethical debates. Religious leaders and organizations may advocate for policies and initiatives that align with their beliefs and values, such as promoting religious education, protecting religious freedom, or addressing social inequality. Although the government is not obliged to follow these recommendations, the influence of religious institutions on public opinion and discourse can impact policy-making processes.

Legal recognition and regulation: Religious institutions are subject to various legal and regulatory requirements, such as registration, taxation, and compliance with labour and safety standards. The Fijian government may establish laws and regulations that govern the operation of religious institutions to ensure transparency, accountability, and adherence to national laws. This legal framework helps to maintain a balance between the autonomy of religious institutions and the government's responsibility to protect the rights and interests of its citizens.

Spiritual Values and Fijian Society

The importance of community, respect, and humility in Fijian culture

Community, respect, and humility are fundamental values in Fijian culture, deeply ingrained in the social fabric and shaping the way people interact with one another. These values contribute to the strong sense of social cohesion, harmony, and unity within Fijian society. The importance of community, respect, and humility in Fijian culture can be described and explained through the following aspects:

Importance of community (Vanua): In Fijian culture, the concept of "vanua" refers to the land, people, and their relationships with one another. The vanua is central to the Fijian way of life, emphasizing the interconnectedness of people, their environment, and their ancestors. This strong sense of community fosters a collective spirit, where individuals prioritize the well-being of the group over personal interests. People support and rely on one another in times of need, celebrating successes together and helping each other through hardships.

Respect for hierarchy and authority: Fijian culture is characterized by a deep respect for hierarchy and authority, with social structures that emphasize the importance of elders, chiefs, and other community leaders. People are expected to show deference and respect to those in positions of authority, acknowledging their wisdom, experience, and leadership. This respect for hierarchy helps maintain social order and harmony within Fijian communities.

Respect for others: Fijians place great importance on treating others with respect, regardless of their social status, age, or background. This respect is expressed through various social customs and etiquette, such as using appropriate titles and honorifics when addressing others and showing consideration and politeness in all interactions. Demonstrating respect for others fosters a sense of unity and harmony within the community, as well as promoting tolerance and understanding among diverse groups.

Humility and modesty: Fijian culture values humility and modesty in personal conduct, discouraging individuals from boasting about their achievements or displaying arrogance. People are expected to be humble and self-effacing, recognizing that their accomplishments are often the result of collective efforts and support from others. This emphasis on humility encourages a sense of shared responsibility and cooperation within the community, as individuals work together for the common good.

Emphasis on relationships and social bonds: Fijian culture places a high value on maintaining strong social bonds and nurturing relationships, both within and outside one's immediate family. People invest time and effort in building and maintaining relationships, participating in communal activities, celebrations, and ceremonies. These social connections contribute to a sense of belonging and support, reinforcing the importance of community and shared identity.

Importance of hospitality and generosity: Fijian culture is known for its warm hospitality and generosity, with people eager to welcome visitors and share their resources with others. This spirit of hospitality reflects the values of community, respect, and humility, as individuals take pride in making others feel welcome and valued.

The concept of "vei lomani" (love and care for one another) and its manifestation in Fijian society

"Vei lomani" is a Fijian concept that translates to "love and care for one another." This cultural value emphasizes the importance of communal bonds, relationships, and mutual support within Fijian society. The concept of vei lomani is deeply ingrained in the Fijian way of life, and its manifestations can be seen in various aspects of their social interactions, community structure, and daily practices.

Communal living: Fijian society is traditionally organized into villages where extended families and clans live closely together. This communal living arrangement fosters strong relationships among community members, who rely on each other for support, guidance, and assistance in times of need.

Social obligations: The concept of vei lomani is expressed through various social obligations and responsibilities that individuals have towards their community. These include participating in communal activities, contributing to village development projects, and assisting with tasks such as house building or farming.

Sharing and generosity: Fijian culture places a high value on sharing resources and helping those in need. The practice of vei lomani encourages community members to share food, material possessions, and labour, fostering a spirit of generosity and cooperation.

Respect and humility: Vei lomani is also evident in the way Fijians interact with each other, showing respect and humility in their social interactions. This includes respecting elders, following social hierarchies, and using polite language when addressing others.

Conflict resolution: The principle of vei lomani plays a significant role in conflict resolution within Fijian communities. It encourages individuals to seek peaceful and harmonious solutions to disputes, often through dialogue, consensus, and compromise.

Celebration and mourning: Vei lomani is displayed during times of celebration and mourning, where communities come together to support one another. In weddings, funerals, and other significant life events, the community plays an essential role in providing emotional and practical support.

Environmental stewardship: The concept of vei lomani extends to the relationship between Fijians and their environment. They view themselves as caretakers of the land and sea, responsible for preserving and protecting their natural resources for future generations. This belief is reflected in their sustainable practices and traditional resource management systems.

The role of spirituality in shaping Fijian values and worldview

Family structures and gender roles

Family structures and gender roles in Fijian culture are deeply rooted in tradition and shaped by social, cultural, and religious norms. Although modernization and globalization have influenced some aspects of family life and gender roles, many Fijian families still adhere to traditional practices and expectations. The following aspects describe and explain family structures and gender roles in Fijian culture:

Extended family structure: In Fijian culture, family structures typically revolve around the extended family, which includes not only the nuclear family (parents and their children) but also grandparents, aunts, uncles, cousins, and other relatives. This extended family system, known as 'tokatoka' or 'mataqali,' is central to Fijian life, providing a strong support network for individuals and ensuring that resources and responsibilities are shared among family members.

Patrilineal system: Fijian society traditionally follows a patrilineal system, where lineage and inheritance are traced through the father's side. The father is considered the head of the family, with authority over decision-making and resource allocation. This system also influences land ownership, with land rights passed down from father to son.

Gender roles: Traditional Fijian culture has distinct gender roles, with men and women expected to fulfill specific duties and responsibilities within the family and community. Men are primarily responsible for providing for the family, engaging in activities such as farming, fishing, and manual labour. Women, on the other hand, take care of the household and children, as well as engaging in activities like weaving, cooking, and gardening.

Traditional marriage practices: In Fijian culture, marriage is considered an important social institution that strengthens bonds between families and communities. Traditionally, arranged marriages were common, with parents selecting suitable partners for their children based on factors such as social status, family connections, and compatibility. While arranged marriages have become less common in modern Fiji, some families still maintain this practice, particularly in more rural and traditional communities.

Respect and gender relations: Fijian culture emphasizes respect and propriety in interactions between men and women. This respect is expressed through social customs and etiquette, such as maintaining a proper distance and using appropriate language when addressing members of the opposite sex. In traditional settings, men and women often socialize separately, with women expected to be modest and deferential in the presence of men.

Changing gender roles and family structures: As Fiji continues to modernize and globalize, there have been shifts in family structures and gender roles, particularly in urban areas and among younger generations. Women are increasingly participating in the workforce and pursuing higher education, leading to more egalitarian relationships within families. These changes have also influenced family structures, with some families adopting a more nuclear model as young people move away from their extended families to pursue education and employment opportunities.

Social hierarchy and status

Social hierarchy and status play a significant role in Fijian culture, with deeply ingrained customs and traditions that emphasize respect for authority and elders. The social structure in Fiji is complex and multifaceted, involving various levels of hierarchy and status that can be understood through the following aspects:

Traditional chiefly system: In Fijian culture, the traditional chiefly system, known as the 'Bose Levu Vakaturaga,' is an important aspect of social hierarchy. Chiefs, or 'turaga,' hold significant authority and are respected as leaders within their communities. The chiefly system is hereditary and often linked to the 'yavusa,' a clan-based system that delineates social status and relationships within a village or community.

Village hierarchy: Fijian villages have their own social hierarchy, with a chief at the top, followed by sub-chiefs, elders, and other village members. The chief holds considerable authority, responsible for decision-making, conflict resolution, and maintaining order within the village. Elders also play an essential role in the village hierarchy, as their wisdom and experience are respected and valued.

Respect for elders: Age is an important factor in determining social status in Fijian culture. Elders are highly respected for their wisdom, experience, and knowledge, and younger individuals are expected to show deference and respect to their elders. This respect is demonstrated through social customs and etiquette, such as using appropriate honorifics and titles when addressing elders and giving priority to them during community gatherings and events.

Land ownership and social status: Land ownership is an essential determinant of social status in Fijian culture, with those who own or control land generally enjoying higher social standing. Land ownership is often linked to the traditional chiefly system and is passed down through generations, ensuring the continuity of social hierarchy and status.

Occupation and education: In contemporary Fijian society, occupation and education are increasingly important factors in determining social status. Those who have pursued higher education or hold professional positions, such as doctors, lawyers, or government officials, often enjoy greater social standing and respect within their communities. This shift reflects the influence of modernization and globalization on Fijian society and the changing dynamics of social hierarchy and status.

Religious leaders: Religious leaders, such as priests, pastors, and imams, also hold a respected position within Fijian society. These leaders are often seen as moral and spiritual guides for their communities, providing counsel and guidance on religious and ethical matters. Their role and influence in the community contribute to their social standing and status.

Interpersonal relationships: Social hierarchy and status in Fijian culture also extend to interpersonal relationships, with individuals expected to show respect and consideration for others based on their age, occupation, and social standing. This respect is expressed through various social customs, such as using appropriate language and gestures when interacting with others and adhering to traditional protocols during community events and ceremonies.

4. CUSTOMS AND TRADITIONS

National and Religious Holidays

In Fijian culture, national and religious holidays play a significant role in marking important historical events, celebrating the country's cultural heritage, and observing various religious traditions. These holidays bring communities together, fostering a sense of unity and shared identity. Some of the main national and religious holidays celebrated in Fiji include:

Fiji Day (October 10): Fiji Day is a national holiday that commemorates Fiji's independence from British colonial rule in 1970. This day is celebrated with various events and activities across the country, including cultural performances, parades, and speeches by government officials. It is an occasion for Fijians to come together and celebrate their national identity and history.

Diwali (October/November): Diwali, also known as the Festival of Lights, is a significant Hindu holiday celebrated by the Indo-Fijian community. This festival marks the victory of light over darkness and good over evil, and is observed with various rituals, such as lighting oil lamps, decorating homes with colourful rangoli designs, and sharing sweets and gifts with family and friends.

Christmas (December 25): Christmas is an important Christian holiday celebrated by Fijian Christians to mark the birth of Jesus Christ. Traditional Christmas celebrations in Fiji involve attending church services, sharing festive meals with family and friends, and exchanging gifts. In some areas, locals participate in singing carols and other festive activities.

Easter (March/April): Easter is another significant Christian holiday observed by Fijians, commemorating the resurrection of Jesus Christ. Easter celebrations typically involve attending church services, participating in special prayers, and spending time with family and friends. Some Fijian communities also observe unique local customs and traditions during Easter, such as the preparation of special foods and the organization of sports events.

Ramadan and Eid al-Fitr (Dates vary according to the Islamic lunar calendar): Ramadan is the holy month of fasting for Muslims, during which they abstain from food and drink from dawn to sunset. At the end of Ramadan, Muslims in Fiji celebrate Eid al-Fitr, a festival that marks the end of the fasting period. This holiday is observed with communal prayers, feasting, and the giving of gifts and charity to those in need.

Prophet Muhammad's Birthday (Dates vary according to the Islamic lunar calendar): Known as Mawlid or Milad-un-Nabi, this Islamic holiday commemorates the birth of the Prophet Muhammad. It is celebrated by Fijian Muslims with special prayers, religious gatherings, and the sharing of food and sweets with family, friends, and neighbours.

New Year's Day (January 1): New Year's Day is a public holiday in Fiji, marking the beginning of the new calendar year. Fijians celebrate this day with various festivities, such as attending parties, organizing family gatherings, and participating in cultural and sporting events.

Traditional ceremonies and celebrations

Fijian culture is rich in traditional ceremonies and celebrations that mark various milestones in life, as well as important cultural and religious events. These ceremonies often involve elaborate rituals, traditional attire, and the sharing of food and kava, a ceremonial drink made from the root of the kava plant. Some notable traditional ceremonies and celebrations in Fijian culture include:

Yaqona (Kava) Ceremony: The Yaqona ceremony is an essential social and cultural event in Fijian culture, where kava is prepared and shared among participants. This ceremony serves as a means of welcoming guests, forging social bonds, and showing respect to elders and chiefs. The ritual involves the preparation of kava by mixing the powdered root with water, then serving it in a traditional wooden bowl called a 'tanoa.'

Sevusevu: The Sevusevu is a formal ceremony of introduction and gift-giving, often performed when visiting a new village or meeting a high-ranking individual for the first time. It typically involves presenting a gift, such as a bundle of kava root, and seeking permission to enter the village or engage with the host. The Sevusevu is an essential custom that demonstrates respect and acknowledges the social hierarchy within Fijian society.

Meke: The Meke is a traditional Fijian dance and storytelling performance that showcases the history, legends, and cultural heritage of the Fijian people. Performed by men and women, the Meke involves chanting, singing, and rhythmic dancing, often accompanied by traditional musical instruments, such as the lali (wooden drum) and the bamboo tube. The Meke is a key element of Fijian celebrations, such as weddings, festivals, and welcoming ceremonies.

Wedding Ceremony: Traditional Fijian weddings are vibrant and colourful celebrations that involve various customs and rituals. These ceremonies often include the exchange of gifts, such as mats, tapa cloth, and whale's teeth (known as 'tabua'), as well as the sharing of food and kava. Traditional attire, including masi (tapa) cloth and salusalu (flower garlands), is commonly worn by the bride, groom, and guests during the celebration.

Birth and Naming Ceremony: In Fijian culture, the birth of a child is an important event marked by various rituals and celebrations. The naming ceremony, known as 'cerevi' or 'vunayasi,' involves the presentation of the child to the community, the bestowing of a name, and the offering of gifts to the child's parents. This ceremony is an essential aspect of Fijian family life and serves to strengthen social bonds within the community.

Funeral Ceremony: Funerals in Fijian culture are significant events that involve various traditional customs and rituals. These ceremonies typically include the preparation of the deceased's body, the sharing of food and kava, and the performance of traditional chants and prayers. Funeral rites vary depending on the social status of the deceased, with more elaborate ceremonies often reserved for chiefs and high-ranking individuals.

First Harvest Celebration: In traditional Fijian communities, the first harvest of crops, such as yams and taro, is an important occasion marked by ceremonies and celebrations. These events involve the offering of the first fruits to the ancestral spirits, seeking their blessings for a bountiful harvest. The first harvest celebration is a communal event, with feasting, dancing, and other festivities bringing the community together.

Food and Culinary Customs

Food and culinary customs in Fijian culture reflect the rich diversity and history of the nation, with influences from Melanesia, Polynesia, India, and China. Fijian cuisine is characterized by the use of local ingredients, such as root vegetables, tropical fruits, seafood, and coconut, along with traditional cooking methods like underground ovens known as 'lovo.' Some key aspects of food and culinary customs in Fijian culture include:

Staple foods: Staple foods in Fijian cuisine include root vegetables like taro (dalo), cassava (tavioka), and yams (uvi), which are often served boiled, steamed, or baked. Rice and breadfruit (uto) are also common staples in the Fijian diet. These staples are usually accompanied by a variety of protein sources, such as fish, seafood, chicken, or pork.

Coconut: Coconut is a versatile and essential ingredient in Fijian cooking, used for its milk, oil, and flesh. Coconut milk is often used to flavour and thicken dishes, such as fish or vegetable curries, while grated coconut is used in desserts and sweets.

Lovo: The lovo is a traditional Fijian cooking method that involves an underground oven, where food is cooked using heated rocks covered with earth. This technique imparts a unique smoky flavour to the food and is typically used during special occasions and communal feasts. Foods commonly cooked in a lovo include marinated meats, fish, and root vegetables, often wrapped in banana or taro leaves.

Kokoda: Kokoda is a popular Fijian dish made from raw fish marinated in lemon or lime juice, which 'cooks' the fish through a process called denaturation. The dish is then mixed with coconut milk, diced vegetables, and chili, resulting in a tangy and refreshing ceviche-like salad.

Indian influence: Due to the significant Indo-Fijian population, Indian cuisine has had a considerable impact on Fijian culinary customs. Dishes like curries, roti (flatbread), and rice-based meals are common, with unique Fijian adaptations that incorporate local ingredients and flavours.

Communal dining: Eating together is an essential aspect of Fijian culture, emphasizing the importance of community and togetherness. Meals are often served family-style, with dishes placed in the centre of the table for everyone to share. In traditional settings, it is common to eat with one's hands, using pieces of roti or cassava to scoop up food.

Kava: Kava, also known as yaqona, is a traditional ceremonial drink made from the ground root of the kava plant. Kava plays a significant role in Fijian culture and is often consumed during social gatherings and important events. The drink is known for its mild sedative effects, promoting relaxation and social bonding among participants.

Etiquette: Proper etiquette is essential during meals in Fijian culture. It is customary to wait for the host or the eldest person present to begin eating before others start. Additionally, it is considered respectful to finish one's meal, as leaving food uneaten may be perceived as unappreciative of the host's efforts.

5. COMMUNICATION STYLES

Verbal and Non-verbal Communication

Verbal and non-verbal communication play crucial roles in Fijian culture, helping to convey emotions, thoughts, and intentions in various social situations. Understanding these communication cues is essential for navigating social interactions and respecting the customs and traditions of the Fijian people.

Verbal communication

Language: Fijian and English are the two official languages of Fiji, with Hindi also widely spoken among the Indo-Fijian population. The Fijian language has various dialects, with Bauan Fijian being the most widely recognized and understood.

Politeness: Fijians are known for their warmth, hospitality, and politeness. It is common to use respectful language when addressing others, particularly elders and those with higher social status. Titles like "Turaga" (chief), or "Momo" (uncle/aunt) are often used to show respect.

Indirect communication: Fijians may communicate indirectly to avoid confrontation or causing discomfort to others. They may use metaphors, stories, or proverbs to convey a message or express their opinion without offending anyone.

Non-verbal communication

Eye contact: In Fijian culture, maintaining direct eye contact, particularly with elders or authority figures, may be considered disrespectful or challenging. It is common to lower one's gaze when speaking to someone of higher status as a sign of respect and humility.

Personal space: Fijians are generally comfortable with close physical proximity during conversations, but it is essential to be aware of one's body language and gestures, as some actions may be considered inappropriate or offensive.

Gestures: Certain gestures hold specific meanings in Fijian culture. For example, pointing with an open hand is considered polite, while pointing with a single finger can be seen as rude. Touching someone's head is also considered disrespectful, as the head is regarded as sacred.

Facial expressions: Fijians may use facial expressions to communicate emotions, approval, or disapproval. For example, a quick lift of the eyebrows may indicate acknowledgment or agreement, while a frown or furrowed brow could signify concern or disapproval.

Posture: Demonstrating respectful posture is important in Fijian culture. When sitting in the presence of elders or high-ranking individuals, it is customary to sit cross-legged, with one's legs tucked under the body (called 'vakatokatoka'). This posture shows respect and humility.

Silence: Silence can also be an important aspect of communication in Fijian culture. It may be used to show respect, convey disagreement, or allow time for reflection and thought. Understanding the context and interpreting the silence correctly is crucial for effective communication in Fijian social situations.

Greetings, Introductions and Titles

Greetings, introductions, and titles in Fijian culture are an essential aspect of social interactions, demonstrating respect, warmth, and hospitality. They help create positive connections with others and set the tone for further communication.

Greetings

Bula: The most common and informal Fijian greeting is "Bula," which translates to "hello" or "welcome." This versatile greeting is used in various contexts, from meeting friends to welcoming visitors.

Ni sa bula vinaka: A more formal greeting is "Ni sa bula vinaka," which means "hello" and is accompanied by a respectful nod. This greeting is often used when addressing elders or those with higher social status.

Time-based greetings: Fijians also use time-based greetings, such as "Yadra" (good morning) and "Ni sa moce" (goodbye or goodnight).

Introductions

Self-introduction: When introducing oneself, it is customary to provide one's name and, if applicable, one's village or family connections. This helps establish common ground and fosters a sense of community and belonging.

Sevusevu: In traditional settings or when visiting a new village, the Sevusevu ceremony is performed. It is a formal introduction that involves presenting a gift, typically a bundle of kava root, to the village chief or host, and seeking permission to enter the village or engage with the host. This ceremony shows respect and acknowledges the social hierarchy within Fijian society.

Titles

Respectful address: Fijians often use titles and honorifics when addressing others to show respect, particularly when speaking to elders or those with higher social status. Some common titles include "Turaga" (chief), "Momo" (uncle/aunt), "Ratu" (chiefly title for men), and "Adi" (chiefly title for women).

Use of names: In general, Fijians prefer to use first names when addressing each other, even in more formal settings. However, it is essential to use respectful titles when addressing elders or those of higher status. It is also polite to ask for permission to use someone's first name if you are unsure of the appropriate title to use.

Physical contact

Handshakes: Handshakes are common in Fijian culture, particularly in formal or business settings. However, the handshake may be more gentle and less firm than in Western cultures. A slight bow or nod of the head while shaking hands can show respect.

Touching: In general, Fijians are more comfortable with physical contact than people from some other cultures. Light touches on the arm or shoulder during conversation are not uncommon. However, touching someone's head is considered disrespectful, as the head is regarded as sacred.

Common expressions and idiomatic phrases

Fijian language, like many other languages, has a wealth of idiomatic expressions and phrases that convey unique cultural insights and colourful ways of communicating. These expressions often reflect Fijian values, beliefs, and traditions. Here are some common expressions and idiomatic phrases in Fijian culture:

"Bula!" – As mentioned previously, "Bula" is a versatile and widely used greeting in Fiji, meaning "hello" or "welcome." It also translates to "life" or "good health" and reflects the warmth and hospitality of Fijian people.

"Vinaka" or *"Vinaka vaka levu"* – "Vinaka" means "thank you," while "Vinaka vaka levu" translates to "thank you very much." These expressions show gratitude and appreciation, essential aspects of Fijian culture.

"Sota tale" – This phrase means "see you again" or "until we meet again." It is used when parting ways with someone, emphasizing the importance of maintaining connections and valuing relationships in Fijian culture.

"Vakamalua" – This term refers to the relaxed, unhurried pace of life in Fiji, often translated as "Fiji time." It implies that there is no need to rush and that things will happen when they are meant to happen.

"Kerekere" – "Kerekere" is a Fijian custom of asking for something without the expectation of repayment. It reflects the communal and supportive nature of Fijian society, where sharing and helping others is highly valued.

"E dua na kena soqo." – This phrase means "a gathering or meeting." It highlights the importance of community and socializing in Fijian culture, emphasizing the value of spending time together and maintaining strong relationships.

"E dua na vanua vakasisila." – Literally translated as "a dirty place," this phrase is used to describe a situation that is complicated or messy, indicating that something is not as it should be.

"Vaka kina na nona i tovo." – This phrase means "to behave according to one's character or nature." It is used to describe someone acting true to their personality or as expected, emphasizing the importance of authenticity and individuality in Fijian culture.

"Na bilo ni yaqona" – Referring to the "kava bowl," this phrase symbolizes unity, community, and hospitality. Sharing a bowl of kava, a traditional ceremonial drink, is a significant social activity in Fiji that brings people together and fosters connections.

"Na ika e rawa na qio." – Translated as "the fish that can catch the shark," this expression is used to describe someone who is resourceful, capable, or able to accomplish great things despite challenging circumstances.

6. BUSINESS ETIQUETTE

Business Culture and Practices

In Fijian culture, business practices and etiquette are influenced by the country's rich traditions and values, emphasizing respect, relationships, and a relaxed approach to time. Understanding these aspects can help create positive business relationships and navigate the Fijian business environment more effectively.

Relationship-building: Fijians value personal connections and trust in business relationships. It is important to invest time in getting to know your business partners, engage in small talk, and be genuinely interested in their lives. Establishing a strong rapport will lay the foundation for a successful business partnership.

Hierarchical structure: Fijian business culture tends to be hierarchical, with decisions often made by senior management. It is crucial to show respect for authority and be aware of the roles and responsibilities within the organization. Make sure to address individuals with their appropriate titles and use a formal approach when necessary.

Communication style: Fijians generally communicate in a polite and indirect manner, using tact and diplomacy to avoid confrontation or causing offense. It is essential to pay attention to non-verbal cues, as they can provide valuable insights into the true feelings or opinions of your counterparts. Be patient and respectful when discussing business matters and avoid applying pressure or being overly assertive.

Punctuality and "Fiji Time": The concept of "Fiji Time" reflects the more relaxed and unhurried approach to time in Fijian culture. While punctuality is appreciated in business settings, it is not uncommon for meetings to start late or be rescheduled. Flexibility and patience are key when dealing with time-sensitive matters in Fiji.

Business attire: In Fiji, business attire is typically more conservative and formal. Men usually wear suits or dress pants with a shirt and tie, while women wear modest dresses or skirts with a blouse. It is important to dress appropriately to show respect and professionalism.

Gift-giving: Exchanging small gifts is a common practice in Fijian business culture, particularly when meeting someone for the first time. The gift should not be overly expensive, as this may cause embarrassment or create an obligation. If you receive a gift, it is customary to reciprocate with a gift of similar value.

Meetings and negotiations: In Fijian business culture, meetings usually begin with informal conversation before transitioning to the main agenda. It is essential to be patient and allow time for relationship-building before diving into business discussions. During negotiations, maintain a respectful and cooperative attitude, and be prepared for decisions to take longer than you might expect.

Hospitality: Fijians are known for their warm and generous hospitality. When invited to a social or business event, it is essential to show appreciation for the invitation and participate in the event wholeheartedly. These occasions are valuable opportunities for relationship-building and networking.

Meeting Etiquette and Negotiations

Meeting etiquette and negotiations in Fijian culture are influenced by the values of respect, relationships, and patience. Understanding these elements can facilitate productive meetings and successful negotiations.

Scheduling meetings: When scheduling meetings, it is advisable to provide ample notice and confirm the appointment a day or two in advance. Avoid scheduling meetings during significant cultural or religious events, as participation in these events is crucial for many Fijians.

Punctuality: While punctuality is appreciated, the concept of "Fiji Time" means that meetings may start late or be rescheduled. It is essential to remain flexible and patient in such situations. If you are running late or need to reschedule, be sure to inform your counterparts as a courtesy.

Greetings: Upon arrival, greet your counterparts with a warm and friendly "Bula" and a handshake. A slight bow or nod of the head while shaking hands can show respect. Use proper titles and address individuals by their first name only if you have permission to do so.

Relationship-building: Meetings in Fijian culture often begin with informal conversation and small talk, allowing participants to build rapport and establish trust. Be prepared to engage in such conversations and ask about your counterparts' well-being, family, or interests before diving into business matters.

Communication style: Fijians tend to communicate in a polite and indirect manner, avoiding confrontation or causing offense. Be respectful, tactful, and diplomatic during discussions, and pay close attention to non-verbal cues, as these can provide valuable insights into the true feelings or opinions of your counterparts.

Decision-making: Fijian business culture is generally hierarchical, with decisions often made by senior management. Be patient and allow time for your counterparts to consult with the necessary decision-makers. Decisions may take longer than expected, so be prepared for this, and avoid applying pressure or being overly assertive.

Negotiations: During negotiations, maintain a respectful and cooperative attitude. Emphasize the benefits of the proposed agreement for both parties and be prepared to compromise. Be cautious with direct criticism, as this may cause offense or damage the relationship. It is essential to remain patient and flexible, as negotiations may take longer than anticipated.

Follow-up: After the meeting, it is crucial to follow up with a summary of the discussions, agreed-upon decisions, and any next steps. This helps maintain the momentum of the negotiations and demonstrates your commitment to the business relationship.

Gift-giving and hospitality

Gift-giving and hospitality are integral parts of Fijian culture, reflecting the values of generosity, respect, and community. Understanding these aspects can help forge stronger relationships and demonstrate appreciation for Fijian customs.

Gift-giving: Exchanging gifts is a common practice in Fijian culture during various occasions such as social visits, business meetings, and traditional ceremonies. Gifts symbolize friendship, gratitude, and respect for the recipient. The focus is on the gesture, not the monetary value of the gift, so it is advisable to avoid overly expensive gifts, as they may cause embarrassment or create an obligation. When offering a gift, use both hands to present it, which signifies respect and thoughtfulness.

Examples of appropriate gifts in Fijian culture include local handicrafts, small souvenirs from your home country, or food items such as chocolates, cookies, or fruits. If you receive a gift, it is customary to reciprocate with a gift of similar value.

Hospitality: Fijians are known for their warm and generous hospitality. When invited to a Fijian home or event, it is essential to show appreciation for the invitation and participate wholeheartedly in the occasion. Bringing a small gift for the host, such as a food item or a modest token from your home country, is a thoughtful gesture.

Dress code: When attending social or cultural events, dress modestly and appropriately. Avoid wearing revealing or casual clothing, as it may be considered disrespectful. For men, wearing a traditional Fijian sulu (a skirt-like garment) is often appreciated, while women can wear a conservative dress or a skirt with a blouse.

Kava ceremony: Kava is a traditional ceremonial drink made from the root of the kava plant. The kava ceremony is an important part of Fijian culture and is often performed during social gatherings, business meetings, or traditional events. Participating in the kava ceremony demonstrates respect for Fijian customs and is a way to connect with your hosts. When offered kava, accept the drink with a smile and clap your hands once before drinking. After finishing, clap your hands three more times to show appreciation.

Dining etiquette: When dining with Fijian hosts, wait for them to invite you to begin eating. It is common for Fijians to eat with their hands, particularly in informal settings. However, utensils will likely be provided for guests. Try to taste all the dishes offered, as this demonstrates appreciation for the host's efforts. It is also polite to leave a small amount of food on your plate to show that you are satisfied and well-fed.

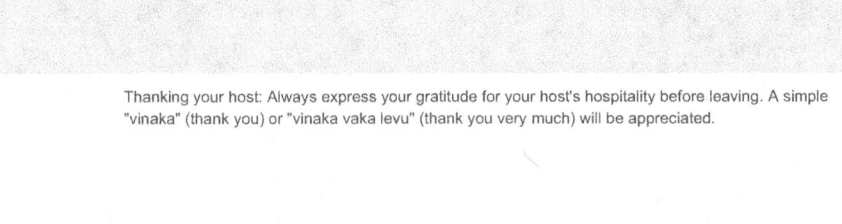

Thanking your host: Always express your gratitude for your host's hospitality before leaving. A simple "vinaka" (thank you) or "vinaka vaka levu" (thank you very much) will be appreciated.

7. SOCIAL ETIQUETTE

Manners and Social Norms

Manners and social norms in Fijian culture are deeply rooted in the values of respect, community, and humility. Understanding these customs can help you navigate social situations and build strong relationships with Fijians.

Respect for elders and authority: Fijian culture places great importance on respecting elders and those in authority. It is essential to show deference to older individuals or those holding leadership positions, whether in a family, a community, or a workplace.

Greetings: When greeting others, use the traditional Fijian greeting "Bula" with a warm and friendly tone. Handshakes are common and should be accompanied by a slight nod or bow of the head to demonstrate respect. Use appropriate titles when addressing others and wait for permission to use first names.

Polite language: Fijians generally communicate in a polite and respectful manner, avoiding confrontation or causing offense. It is important to be tactful and diplomatic in conversations and pay attention to non-verbal cues.

Modesty in dress: Dress modestly and conservatively to show respect for Fijian customs. Avoid wearing revealing or overly casual clothing, particularly when visiting villages, attending cultural events, or meeting with elders.

Removing shoes: When entering a Fijian home or a sacred space, it is customary to remove your shoes as a sign of respect. Be prepared to sit on the floor, often on woven mats, during social gatherings or ceremonies.

Tabua (whale's tooth): The tabua is a sacred cultural symbol in Fiji and is often used during ceremonies and as a gift to show deep respect. It is essential to treat a tabua with the utmost reverence if you are presented with one.

Personal space and touching: In Fijian culture, maintaining an appropriate distance during conversations is important. Unnecessary physical contact, especially between opposite sexes, should be avoided. Public displays of affection are generally frowned upon.

Respect for the "vanua": The concept of "vanua" (land) holds significant spiritual importance in Fijian culture. Show respect for the land and natural environment by following local customs and guidelines, including seeking permission to enter certain areas, participating in traditional ceremonies, and refraining from littering.

Sharing and generosity: Fijian culture values community and sharing. Be prepared to participate in communal activities and contribute to the group, whether by sharing food, resources, or time.

Accepting invitations: When invited to a Fijian home or event, accept the invitation graciously and participate fully in the gathering. Be sure to thank your host for their hospitality and, if possible, reciprocate with an invitation of your own.

Dining Etiquette and Table Manners

Dining etiquette and table manners in Fijian culture reflect the values of respect, community, and hospitality. Understanding these customs can help you navigate mealtimes and enjoy the shared experience of dining with Fijians.

Seating arrangements: In traditional Fijian gatherings, people often sit on the floor, typically on woven mats. Guests are usually seated according to their age or status, with elders and individuals of higher status seated in more prominent positions. Be sure to wait for your host to show you where to sit.

Handwashing: In many Fijian homes, it is customary to wash hands before and after a meal, particularly when eating with your hands. Your host may provide a bowl of water for this purpose. Be sure to follow their lead.

Starting the meal: Wait for your host to invite you to start eating or say a prayer before the meal. It is considered impolite to begin eating before everyone is seated or before the host gives the signal to start.

Eating with hands: While utensils are often provided, particularly in urban settings, it is common for Fijians to eat with their hands, especially in informal settings. If you choose to eat with your hands, use your right hand for picking up food, as the left hand is considered unclean. Follow your host's lead and be mindful of the cultural norms.

Trying different dishes: It is polite to sample a bit of each dish offered. Compliment the host on the meal and express your appreciation for their efforts. If you have dietary restrictions, inform your host in advance, or politely decline certain dishes, explaining your reasons.

Serving portions: In Fijian culture, it is customary to serve more food than can be consumed. Leaving a small amount of food on your plate is considered polite, as it indicates that you are satisfied and well-fed.

Drinking kava: Kava is a traditional ceremonial drink made from the root of the kava plant. If you are offered kava, accept it graciously and participate in the ceremony as a sign of respect for Fijian customs.

Conversation: Engage in light conversation and small talk during the meal. Fijians appreciate a relaxed and friendly atmosphere during meals. Avoid discussing sensitive or controversial topics.

Toasts and speeches: Toasts and speeches may be given during more formal dinners or special occasions. If you are invited to make a toast or speech, keep it brief and express your gratitude and appreciation for the host's hospitality.

Thanking your host: Always thank your host for the meal and their hospitality before leaving. A simple "vinaka" (thank you) or "vinaka vaka levu" (thank you very much) will be appreciated.

Dress Code and Appearance

Dress code and appearance in Fijian culture are deeply rooted in values of respect, modesty, and cultural sensitivity. Understanding the customs surrounding dress and appearance can help you navigate social situations and demonstrate respect for Fijian traditions.

Modest clothing: Fijians generally dress modestly, particularly in rural areas and villages. Revealing or overly casual clothing is considered inappropriate and disrespectful. It is essential to cover your shoulders, knees, and midriff in most situations, especially when visiting villages, attending cultural events, or meeting with elders.

Traditional attire: Fijian men often wear a sulu, a traditional skirt-like garment, for both casual and formal occasions. Sulu can be worn with a shirt, and in more formal settings, a suit jacket. Women traditionally wear a conservative dress, a skirt with a blouse, or a sulu paired with a blouse. Wearing traditional Fijian attire as a visitor is often appreciated and seen as a sign of respect for the local culture.

Urban areas: In urban areas like Suva, Nadi, and Lautoka, the dress code is generally more relaxed, and you will find a mix of Western and traditional clothing. However, it is still crucial to dress modestly and appropriately, especially when visiting places of worship, attending ceremonies, or meeting with elders.

Beachwear: Swimwear, such as swimsuits and bikinis, should be reserved for the beach or swimming pool areas. When walking to and from the beach or pool, cover up with a sarong, shorts, or a light shirt to show respect for local customs.

Footwear: Removing shoes before entering a Fijian home or sacred space is customary. When visiting villages, it is a good idea to wear comfortable, easy-to-remove shoes or sandals.

Attire for religious places: When visiting places of worship, such as churches, temples, or mosques, dress conservatively and respectfully. For women, this often means covering your head, shoulders, and legs. For men, wearing long pants and a shirt with sleeves is appropriate.

Business attire: In a business setting, Fijians typically dress formally. Men should wear a suit and tie, while women should wear a conservative dress, skirt and blouse, or a pantsuit. Traditional attire, such as a sulu, is also acceptable for both men and women in some business settings.

Appearance and grooming: Fijians value cleanliness and neatness in personal appearance. Ensure that your clothing is clean and well-maintained, and practice good personal hygiene. Avoid wearing excessive jewellery or accessories, as it may be perceived as ostentatious.

8. BODY LANGUAGE AND PERSONAL SPACE

Gestures and facial expressions

Gestures and facial expressions in Fijian culture reflect the values of respect, humility, and non-confrontation. Understanding these non-verbal cues can help you navigate social situations and communicate more effectively with Fijians.

Eye contact: Moderate eye contact is appreciated in Fijian culture. While maintaining eye contact shows attentiveness and respect, avoid staring or holding eye contact for too long, as it may be perceived as aggressive or impolite.

Smiling: Fijians are known for their warmth and friendliness, often greeting others with a broad smile. Smiling is an essential aspect of communication in Fijian culture, as it conveys a sense of openness and approachability.

Nodding and head movements: Nodding your head slightly while listening or speaking is a sign of agreement and attentiveness. However, be aware that the side-to-side headshake, which may indicate 'no' in many cultures, can sometimes mean 'yes' in Fijian culture. Pay attention to the context and accompanying verbal cues to understand the intended meaning.

Gesturing: Fijians use hand gestures to convey meaning and emphasize points during conversations. However, it is important to use gestures moderately and avoid overly animated expressions, as they may be perceived as aggressive or disrespectful.

Pointing: Pointing directly at someone or something with your index finger is considered impolite in Fijian culture. Instead, use your whole hand or nod your head in the direction you want to indicate.

Crossing arms and legs: In some situations, crossing your arms or legs may be seen as a sign of defiance, disrespect, or disinterest. Be aware of your body language and posture, particularly when in the presence of elders or authority figures.

Touching: Fijians generally maintain personal space during conversations and avoid unnecessary physical contact, especially between members of the opposite sex. Public displays of affection are generally frowned upon.

Silence and pauses: Fijians may use silence and pauses during conversations to reflect, think, or show respect. Do not feel the need to fill every pause with words; instead, embrace the silence and use it as an opportunity to listen and understand.

Showing respect to elders and authority figures: When in the presence of an elder or someone with authority, it is essential to show respect through your gestures, facial expressions, and body language. This may include bowing your head slightly, speaking softly, and avoiding direct eye contact.

Personal Space and Touch

Personal space and touch in Fijian culture are influenced by values of respect, modesty, and sensitivity to others' comfort. Understanding these aspects of Fijian culture can help you navigate social interactions and demonstrate respect for local customs.

Personal space: Fijians generally maintain a comfortable distance during conversations, respecting each other's personal space. While personal space expectations may vary depending on the relationship between individuals, it is essential to observe and respect the personal space of others, especially when interacting with people of the opposite sex or individuals you are not well acquainted with.

Physical contact: In general, Fijians are not overly touchy-feely, particularly between members of the opposite sex. It is important to avoid unnecessary physical contact or gestures that may be perceived as too intimate, such as hugging, touching someone's arm, or placing your hand on someone's shoulder, unless you have a close relationship with the person.

Greeting etiquette: When greeting someone, a firm handshake accompanied by a smile and eye contact is appropriate for both men and women. In some cases, particularly among close friends or family members, a gentle hug or cheek-to-cheek touch may be acceptable. Be sure to follow the lead of your Fijian counterparts in determining the appropriate level of physical contact during greetings.

Public displays of affection: Public displays of affection, such as holding hands, hugging, or kissing, are generally frowned upon in Fijian culture, especially in rural areas and villages. Keep physical affection private and maintain a respectful demeanour in public.

Touching the head: The head is considered sacred in Fijian culture, and touching someone's head without permission is considered disrespectful. Refrain from patting or touching someone's head, including children.

Gender dynamics: Be particularly mindful of personal space and physical contact when interacting with individuals of the opposite sex, as Fijian society tends to be conservative in this regard. Men and women typically maintain a respectful distance from each other, and physical contact is limited to avoid misunderstandings or discomfort.

Eye contact and body posture

Eye contact and body posture play essential roles in communication and conveying respect in Fijian culture. Understanding these non-verbal cues can help you navigate social situations and interact more effectively with Fijians.

Eye contact: Moderate eye contact is valued in Fijian culture, as it demonstrates attentiveness, sincerity, and respect. However, excessive or prolonged eye contact may be perceived as intrusive or even aggressive. When speaking with someone, maintain eye contact to show your interest, but be sure to break it occasionally to avoid making the other person feel uncomfortable.

Body posture: Fijians appreciate a relaxed and respectful body posture during conversations. Stand or sit up straight, as slouching may be interpreted as a sign of disrespect or disinterest. Keep your arms relaxed by your sides or in your lap, and avoid crossing your arms, which can be perceived as defensive or standoffish.

Showing respect to elders and authority figures: In the presence of elders or authority figures, it is essential to demonstrate respect through your body posture. Bow your head slightly, maintain a respectful distance, and avoid staring directly into their eyes for an extended period. Speaking softly and using a humble tone of voice can further convey your respect.

Feet and sitting positions: In traditional Fijian settings, such as in villages or when sitting on the floor, be mindful of your feet's position. Pointing your feet directly at someone or a sacred object is considered disrespectful. Instead, tuck your feet under you, sit cross-legged, or adopt a position that does not direct your feet toward others.

Personal space: Maintain an appropriate distance during conversations to respect others' personal space. Standing too close to someone may be perceived as invasive or disrespectful. Be particularly mindful of personal space when interacting with individuals of the opposite sex.

9. EDUCATION AND THE ARTS

Education System and Values

Education is highly valued in Fijian culture, as it is seen as a key factor in personal development, social mobility, and contributing to the community and the nation. The educational system in Fiji is influenced by its colonial history and cultural values, reflecting a blend of British and local traditions.

Structure of the educational system: The Fijian education system is divided into four main stages: early childhood education, primary education, secondary education, and tertiary education. Primary education is compulsory and free for children between the ages of 6 and 14. The system is based on a British model, with English as the medium of instruction, and it incorporates elements of Fijian culture and history.

Early childhood education: This stage is optional and typically caters to children between the ages of 3 and 5. Kindergartens and pre-schools provide early childhood education, focusing on developing basic social, cognitive, and motor skills.

Primary education: Primary education lasts for eight years, from Year 1 to Year 8. The curriculum covers core subjects like English, mathematics, science, social studies, and physical education, as well as Fijian or Hindi (depending on the student's ethnic background) and moral education, which emphasizes values such as respect, responsibility, and cooperation.

Secondary education: Secondary education lasts for six years, divided into two stages: lower secondary (Years 9-10) and upper secondary (Years 11-13). Students take a range of subjects, including core subjects and electives, such as vocational courses or foreign languages. At the end of Year 10, students sit for the Fiji Year 10 Certificate Examination, and at the end of Year 12, they take the Fiji Year 12 Certificate Examination. After completing Year 13, students can sit for the Fiji Year 13 Certificate Examination, which determines their eligibility for university entrance.

Tertiary education: Tertiary education in Fiji includes universities, technical colleges, and vocational training institutions. The University of the South Pacific, Fiji National University, and the University of Fiji are the main higher education providers in the country. Students can pursue a variety of degree programs, including undergraduate, postgraduate, and vocational courses.

Educational values: Fijian culture places a strong emphasis on respect, discipline, humility, and community engagement. These values are often integrated into the educational system through classroom expectations, extracurricular activities, and moral education. Education is seen as a means to uplift the community and contribute to the nation's development.

Access to education: While Fiji has made significant progress in providing education to its citizens, challenges remain, particularly in rural areas where access to quality education can be limited. The Fijian government has implemented various initiatives to improve access to education, such as providing scholarships, upgrading school facilities, and investing in teacher training.

Literature, music, and the visual arts

Fijian culture has a rich and diverse history in literature, music, and the visual arts, which reflects the nation's unique blend of indigenous traditions, colonial influences, and multicultural heritage.

Literature: Fijian literature includes traditional oral storytelling, poetry, legends, and myths, as well as contemporary works of fiction and non-fiction. Storytelling and reciting poetry have been vital aspects of Fijian culture for centuries, often used to share history, values, and life lessons. With the introduction of the written word, many Fijian authors have published works that explore themes such as identity, colonialism, migration, and cultural preservation. Notable Fijian authors include Epeli Hau'ofa, Satendra Nandan, and Albert Wendt.

Music: Music is an integral part of Fijian culture and is used for entertainment, storytelling, and ritual ceremonies. Traditional Fijian music is characterized by vocal harmonies, percussion, and the use of indigenous instruments such as the lali (a wooden drum), bamboo flutes, and panpipes. Popular contemporary music genres in Fiji include reggae, gospel, and Fijian pop, which often incorporate traditional musical elements. The meke, a traditional Fijian dance, is performed on special occasions and accompanied by singing and rhythmic drumming.

Visual arts: Fijian visual arts encompass a wide range of traditional and contemporary practices, including carving, weaving, pottery, and painting. Traditional Fijian art is characterized by its intricate craftsmanship and the use of natural materials, such as wood, barkcloth, and fibres.

Carving: Wood carving is a longstanding tradition in Fijian culture, with skilled artisans creating ornate sculptures, masks, and ceremonial objects. Some of the most famous Fijian carvings include the cannibal forks (iculanibokola), used in ritual ceremonies, and the tabua, a whale's-tooth used as a prestigious gift and symbol of social status.

Weaving: Weaving is another essential aspect of Fijian visual arts, with women traditionally weaving mats, baskets, and clothing from pandanus leaves, coconut fibres, and other plant materials. The masi, or tapa cloth, is a particularly significant art form, made from the inner bark of the paper mulberry tree and decorated with geometric patterns and symbolic motifs.

Pottery: Fijian pottery is characterized by its simple yet functional design, with traditional pottery techniques passed down through generations. Pottery is used to create cooking and storage vessels, as well as decorative items.

Painting: Contemporary Fijian painters draw on traditional themes and techniques while exploring modern subjects and styles. Notable Fijian painters include Epeli Hau'ofa, Anare Somumu, and Lambert Ho.

Popular culture and media

Popular culture and media in Fijian culture encompass a diverse array of entertainment forms, news sources, and platforms that reflect the nation's multicultural identity and evolving social landscape.

Television and Radio: Fiji has several television channels, including the state-owned Fiji Broadcasting Corporation (FBC) and private broadcasters such as Fiji Television Limited (Fiji TV). These channels offer a mix of local and international content, including news, sports, dramas, comedies, and documentaries. Radio stations in Fiji cater to different languages (English, Fijian, and Hindi) and musical tastes, featuring news, talk shows, and various music genres.

Print Media: Newspapers and magazines play an essential role in informing the Fijian population about current events, politics, and culture. Major newspapers in Fiji include the Fiji Times and the Fiji Sun, which are published in English. Additionally, there are Hindi-language newspapers such as Shanti Dut and local-language periodicals that cater to different communities and interests.

Cinema: The Fijian film industry is relatively small but growing, with local filmmakers producing documentaries, short films, and feature films that explore various aspects of Fijian culture, history, and contemporary issues. International films are also popular in Fiji, with several cinemas screening Hollywood, Bollywood, and other foreign movies.

Sports: Sports play a significant role in Fijian popular culture, with rugby being the national sport and a source of immense pride. Both rugby union and rugby sevens are widely followed, with the Fiji national team often performing well in international competitions. Other popular sports include soccer, netball, cricket, and athletics.

Festivals and Events: Throughout the year, various cultural and entertainment events take place in Fiji, celebrating the nation's rich heritage and diverse communities. Some notable festivals include the Hibiscus Festival, the Bula Festival, and the Fiji International Jazz and Blues Festival, which showcase music, dance, food, and other aspects of Fijian culture.

Social Media and the Internet: With increasing internet penetration, social media platforms such as Facebook, Twitter, and Instagram have become popular among Fijians, particularly among the younger generation. These platforms are used for communication, entertainment, and sharing information on news, events, and cultural topics. Online news outlets and blogs also provide alternative sources of information and perspectives on Fijian society.

Music and Dance: As mentioned earlier, music is an essential aspect of Fijian culture, with traditional and contemporary styles enjoyed by many. Fijian pop music often incorporates elements of reggae, gospel, and indigenous music, appealing to a broad audience. Dance clubs and live music venues provide entertainment and opportunities for socializing.

10. PRACTICAL TIPS FOR TRAVELLERS AND EXPATS

Safety and Security Tips

While Fiji is generally a safe and welcoming country for visitors, it's essential to be aware of safety and security tips to ensure a pleasant stay. Following these guidelines will help you navigate Fijian culture respectfully and avoid any potential issues:

Respect local customs and traditions: Fijian culture places great importance on respect and humility. Be mindful of local customs, such as dress codes, social norms, and etiquette. For example, when visiting villages, it's appropriate to dress modestly, cover shoulders and knees, and remove hats and sunglasses.

Be cautious in urban areas: As in any country, urban areas can have higher crime rates than rural areas. Be vigilant when exploring cities, especially at night, and avoid walking alone in poorly lit or unfamiliar areas. Keep your belongings secure and avoid displaying valuables openly.

Use reputable transportation: When using taxis or other forms of transportation, choose well-established and reputable providers. If possible, ask for recommendations from your hotel or local contacts.

Observe water safety: Fiji has beautiful beaches and water activities, but be cautious when swimming, snorkelling, or diving. Always swim with a buddy, avoid swimming in strong currents or rough seas, and follow the advice of local authorities or experienced guides.

Be aware of natural hazards: Fiji is located in a region prone to tropical cyclones and earthquakes. Stay informed about any potential weather events or natural hazards during your visit and follow the advice of local authorities in case of emergencies.

Follow health precautions: Protect yourself from mosquito-borne illnesses such as dengue fever by using insect repellent and wearing long sleeves and pants when outdoors. Also, practice good hygiene and avoid consuming tap water, opting for bottled water instead.

Respect local wildlife: When exploring Fiji's natural environment, maintain a safe distance from animals and plants, and avoid touching or disturbing them. Some animals and plants can be dangerous or poisonous, so exercise caution and follow the guidance of local experts.

Avoid political gatherings: As a visitor, it's best to avoid engaging in political discussions or attending political events, as they can sometimes become contentious.

Seek local advice: If you're unsure about any aspect of Fijian culture or safety, don't hesitate to ask locals, hotel staff, or tour guides for advice. They will often provide helpful information to ensure your safety and enjoyment.

Transportation and accommodation

When visiting or living in Fiji, it's essential to keep in mind some practical tips regarding transportation and accommodation. These tips will help you navigate the country more efficiently and comfortably:

Transportation

Air travel: Nadi International Airport is the primary entry point for international flights, while Nausori International Airport, near Suva, serves some regional flights. For domestic travel, Fiji Airways and Northern Air operate regular flights between the main islands and some smaller ones.

Taxis: Taxis are widely available in urban areas and at airports. Ensure you use licensed taxis and agree on a fare before starting your journey. Many taxis have meters, but some may not, so it's good to negotiate the fare upfront.

Buses: Local buses are a cost-effective way to travel around Fiji, especially on the main islands of Viti Levu and Vanua Levu. Buses come in various types, from standard coaches to open-window buses, known as "carrier buses."

Rental cars: If you prefer more independence, renting a car is an option. Major international rental agencies, such as Avis and Budget, have offices in Fiji. Make sure you have a valid driver's license and are familiar with local road rules.

Ferries and boats: To travel between islands, ferries and boats are available. Main routes include connections between Viti Levu, Vanua Levu, Taveuni, and the Yasawa and Mamanuca island groups. Ferry services can be affected by weather conditions, so it's crucial to check schedules in advance and book accordingly.

Accommodation

Hotels and resorts: Fiji offers a wide range of accommodation options, from luxury resorts to budget hotels. Popular tourist areas, such as Denarau Island, the Coral Coast, and the Mamanuca and Yasawa islands, have numerous hotels and resorts catering to different budgets and preferences.

Hostels and guesthouses: For budget travellers, hostels and guesthouses are available throughout Fiji, offering dormitory-style rooms or private accommodations at affordable rates. Some also provide shared kitchen facilities and common areas for socializing.

Homestays and village stays: To experience authentic Fijian culture, consider staying in a local village or participating in a homestay. This type of accommodation allows you to immerse yourself in the local community, learn about traditional customs, and enjoy home-cooked meals.

Vacation rentals: If you prefer more privacy or plan to stay for an extended period, vacation rentals, such as apartments or villas, can be a suitable option. Websites like Airbnb, Booking.com, and VRBO offer various listings in Fiji.

Booking and planning: To secure the best deals and avoid disappointment, book your accommodation well in advance, especially during peak travel seasons. Research the location, facilities, and reviews to ensure your chosen accommodation meets your needs and expectations.

Healthcare and insurance

Access to quality healthcare and insurance is essential for travellers and expats in any country, including Fiji. Here are some practical tips to ensure you have a safe and healthy stay:

Healthcare:

Public vs. private healthcare: Fiji has a mix of public and private healthcare facilities. Public hospitals and clinics can be found in urban areas and larger towns, providing basic medical services at low or no cost. However, public healthcare in Fiji may be limited in resources and staffing and wait times can be long. Private clinics and hospitals, on the other hand, offer a higher standard of care but at a higher cost.

Medical evacuation: In case of a severe illness or injury requiring specialized treatment, medical evacuation to a nearby country, such as Australia or New Zealand, may be necessary. This can be expensive, so it's crucial to have appropriate insurance coverage.

Pharmacies and medication: Pharmacies can be found in urban areas and larger towns, but the availability of medications may be limited. It's a good idea to bring a sufficient supply of any prescription medications you may need, as well as a copy of the prescription.

Vaccinations and preventive measures: Before traveling to Fiji, consult your healthcare provider to ensure you have the recommended vaccinations, such as Hepatitis A, Typhoid, and Tetanus. Also, take precautions against mosquito-borne diseases, such as dengue fever and Zika virus, by using insect repellent and wearing protective clothing.

Food and water safety: To avoid gastrointestinal issues, practice good hygiene and be cautious with food and water. Drink bottled or filtered water, avoid ice made from tap water, and consume well-cooked food from reputable establishments.

Insurance:

Travel insurance: Before traveling to Fiji, ensure you have adequate travel insurance that covers medical expenses, evacuation, and repatriation. Be sure to read the policy carefully to understand the coverage and any exclusions.

International health insurance: For expats planning a longer stay in Fiji, consider purchasing international health insurance. This type of insurance typically covers a more comprehensive range of medical services and can be tailored to your specific needs.

Insurance for adventure activities: If you plan on participating in adventure sports or activities, such as scuba diving or hiking, make sure your insurance policy covers these. Some policies may require additional coverage for high-risk activities.

Emergency contacts and assistance: Keep a list of emergency contacts, including your insurance provider's assistance hotline, local hospitals or clinics, and your country's embassy or consulate in Fiji.

11. OVERCOMING STEREOTYPES AND PREJUDICES

Common Misconceptions and Stereotypes

Fiji, like any other country, is subject to misconceptions and stereotypes that may not accurately represent its people, culture, or environment. Here are some common misconceptions and stereotypes about Fiji:

Fiji is only for honeymooners and luxury travellers: While Fiji is famous for its romantic getaways and luxury resorts, it offers a diverse range of experiences for travellers with different interests and budgets. Fiji has various accommodations, from budget-friendly hostels to mid-range hotels, and offers a range of activities such as hiking, cultural experiences, and water sports, catering to various travellers.

Fiji is just one island: Fiji is an archipelago comprising over 330 islands, with approximately 110 of them inhabited. Viti Levu and Vanua Levu are the two largest islands, but many smaller islands are also worth exploring, such as the Mamanucas, Yasawas, and Taveuni.

Fijians only wear grass skirts and live in traditional huts: While Fijian culture and traditions are an essential aspect of the country, Fiji has a diverse and modern society. Fijians wear contemporary clothing and live in a variety of homes, ranging from traditional village houses to modern apartments in urban areas.

Fiji is always sunny and warm: While Fiji is known for its tropical climate and beautiful beaches, it also experiences a rainy season (typically from November to April) with occasional tropical cyclones. Weather can vary across the islands, so it's essential to check the local forecast and plan accordingly.

Fiji is an unsafe destination: Fiji is generally a safe destination for travellers, but as with any country, it's essential to take precautions and be aware of your surroundings. Petty crime can occur, particularly in urban areas, so be vigilant and follow general travel safety tips.

Fiji has limited cultural diversity: Fiji has a rich cultural heritage, with a diverse population that includes indigenous Fijians, Indo-Fijians, and smaller communities of Europeans, Chinese, and other Pacific Islanders. This diversity is reflected in the country's customs, languages, religions, and cuisines.

All Fijians are Christian: While Christianity is the predominant religion in Fiji, the country is home to various religious communities, including Hindus, Muslims, and followers of traditional indigenous beliefs. Fiji is known for its religious tolerance, and interfaith dialogue is an essential aspect of the nation's harmony.

Strategies for overcoming biases and promoting understanding

Overcoming stereotypes and prejudices is essential for promoting understanding and fostering positive relationships in Fiji and beyond. Here are some strategies to help you overcome biases and embrace a more inclusive perspective:

Educate yourself: Learn about Fiji's history, culture, and people from reliable sources. Understanding the complexities of the country's demographics and cultural heritage will help you overcome stereotypes and appreciate the richness of Fijian society.

Engage in open dialogue: Engage in conversations with Fijians from different backgrounds and be open to listening and learning from their perspectives. This will help challenge your assumptions and deepen your understanding of Fiji's diverse communities.

Be aware of your own biases: Recognize and acknowledge your own stereotypes and prejudices. Reflect on how they may have been formed and how they might be influencing your perceptions and interactions with others.

Foster empathy and understanding: Put yourself in the shoes of others and try to understand their experiences and viewpoints. This will help you build connections and appreciate the unique aspects of Fiji's diverse communities.

Challenge stereotypes and prejudices: When you encounter stereotypes or prejudiced statements, speak up and challenge them. Provide accurate information and share your own experiences to promote understanding.

Promote cultural exchange: Participate in cultural events, workshops, or activities that foster intercultural exchange and understanding. This will help you learn about the customs, traditions, and values of different Fijian communities.

Encourage inclusivity: Advocate for inclusivity and equal opportunities for all Fijians, regardless of their background. By supporting policies and initiatives that promote social cohesion, you can contribute to a more harmonious society.

Travel and immerse yourself in the culture: Visit different parts of Fiji, engage with local communities, and participate in traditional activities to gain a deeper understanding of the culture and customs. This first-hand experience will help break down stereotypes and foster appreciation for the country's diversity.

Share positive stories: Share your own experiences and stories that highlight the richness of Fijian culture and the warmth of its people. Encourage others to do the same and promote positive narratives that challenge stereotypes.

Be a role model: Demonstrate openness, respect, and understanding in your interactions with others. Your behaviour can influence those around you and help create a more inclusive environment.

12. BUILDING CROSS-CULTURAL RELATIONSHIPS

Effective Communication and Conflict Resolution

Building cross-cultural relationships is essential for effective communication and conflict resolution in any multicultural society, including Fiji. Here are some tips to help you develop strong cross-cultural relationships and foster understanding:

Develop cultural awareness: Learn about Fiji's history, culture, customs, values, and beliefs. Understanding the various cultural nuances will enable you to communicate more effectively and avoid misunderstandings.

Be open-minded and respectful: Approach interactions with an open mind and a willingness to learn from others. Show respect for different viewpoints, beliefs, and customs, even if they differ from your own.

Practice active listening: Make a conscious effort to listen attentively and empathetically to others. This will help you understand their perspectives, emotions, and needs, and foster a stronger connection.

Be mindful of non-verbal communication: In addition to words, consider the tone of voice, facial expressions, body language, and gestures used in communication. These non-verbal cues can provide valuable insight into the emotions and intentions of others.

Adapt your communication style: Recognize that different cultures may have different communication styles and preferences. Be flexible and adapt your communication style to suit the context and the individual you are interacting with.

Seek clarification: If you are unsure about the meaning or intention behind a statement, ask for clarification. This can help prevent misunderstandings and conflicts.

Establish trust: Building trust is crucial for effective communication and conflict resolution. Be honest, transparent, and consistent in your actions and communication to foster trust and credibility.

Show appreciation and gratitude: Acknowledge the contributions and efforts of others and express your gratitude. This can help strengthen relationships and foster a positive atmosphere.

Be patient and tolerant: Building cross-cultural relationships takes time and effort. Be patient and allow for the possibility of misunderstandings or miscommunications. Practice tolerance and understanding as you navigate cultural differences.

Engage in conflict resolution: When conflicts arise, address them in a timely and respectful manner. Use effective communication, active listening, and problem-solving skills to find a mutually acceptable resolution. Be willing to compromise and find common ground.

Participate in cultural events and activities: Engaging in cultural events and activities can provide valuable opportunities to interact with people from different backgrounds, learn about their customs and traditions, and build relationships.

Encourage teamwork and collaboration: Promote a collaborative environment in which people from different cultural backgrounds can work together, share ideas, and learn from each other. This will help create a sense of unity and foster strong cross-cultural relationships.

Adapting to cultural differences

Adapting to cultural differences in Fiji is essential for making the most of your time in the country, whether you're a traveller, expat, or working with Fijians. Here are some tips to help you adapt to cultural differences in Fiji:

Educate yourself: Learn about Fijian history, culture, customs, values, and beliefs. Familiarize yourself with local etiquette, social norms, and communication styles. This will help you avoid misunderstandings and navigate cultural differences more effectively.

Be open-minded and curious: Approach new experiences with an open mind and a willingness to learn. Embrace the differences you encounter and seek opportunities to learn from Fijians and their culture.

Observe and imitate: Watch how locals interact with each other and handle various situations. Adopting appropriate behaviours and following local customs can help you fit in and feel more comfortable in Fiji.

Ask questions: If you're unsure about something, don't be afraid to ask questions. Fijians are generally friendly and welcoming, and they will likely appreciate your interest in their culture.

Show respect: Show respect for Fijian customs, traditions, and beliefs, even if they differ from your own. Be mindful of your actions and language to ensure you do not offend anyone.

Be flexible and adaptable: Be prepared to adjust your behaviour, communication style, and expectations to suit the local context. This flexibility will help you navigate cultural differences more smoothly and enhance your interactions with Fijians.

Build relationships: Develop friendships and connections with Fijians from diverse backgrounds. These relationships will enrich your experience in Fiji and provide valuable insights into local culture.

Participate in cultural activities: Attend local events, festivals, and ceremonies to experience Fijian culture firsthand. This will deepen your understanding of the culture and help you adapt more effectively.

Learn the local language: Although English is widely spoken in Fiji, learning some basic Fijian or Fiji Hindi phrases can help you connect with locals and demonstrate your respect for their culture.

Reflect on your own culture and biases: Recognize that you bring your own cultural biases and assumptions with you. Reflecting on these can help you better understand and appreciate the cultural differences you encounter in Fiji.

Be patient: Adapting to a new culture takes time and effort. Be patient with yourself and others as you adjust to the differences in Fiji.

Developing empathy and cultural intelligence

Developing empathy and cultural intelligence is crucial for understanding and appreciating the diverse culture of Fiji. Here are some steps to help you enhance your empathy and cultural intelligence while in Fiji:

Learn about Fijian culture: Invest time in understanding Fiji's history, traditions, customs, values, and beliefs. This knowledge will help you appreciate the cultural nuances and make sense of the behaviours and attitudes you encounter.

Engage with locals: Interact with Fijians from different backgrounds to learn about their perspectives, experiences, and values. Engaging in conversations and participating in local activities can help you develop empathy and deepen your understanding of Fijian culture.

Be open-minded and non-judgmental: Approach new experiences with an open mind and avoid making quick judgments. Embrace differences and try to understand the underlying reasons behind certain behaviours or customs.

Reflect on your own culture and biases: Recognize your own cultural biases, stereotypes, and assumptions. Reflecting on these can help you better understand and appreciate cultural differences and develop empathy for others.

Practice active listening: Listen attentively and empathetically to others, trying to understand their feelings, thoughts, and experiences. This will help you connect with Fijians on a deeper level and foster empathy.

Observe and learn: Pay attention to the non-verbal cues, body language, and communication styles of Fijians. Observing and learning from locals can help you improve your cultural intelligence and adapt to different situations more effectively.

Develop emotional intelligence: Cultivate self-awareness, self-regulation, motivation, empathy, and social skills. These emotional intelligence competencies can help you navigate cultural differences and interact with others more effectively.

Be flexible and adaptable: Be willing to adjust your behaviour, communication style, and expectations to suit the local context. This flexibility will help you develop cultural intelligence and improve your interactions with Fijians.

Seek feedback: Ask for feedback from Fijians on your behaviour, communication, and understanding of their culture. This feedback can help you identify areas for improvement and enhance your cultural intelligence.

Learn from your experiences: Reflect on your experiences in Fiji and identify the lessons you've learned about empathy and cultural intelligence. Apply these lessons to future interactions and continue to grow and develop as a culturally intelligent individual.

13. CASE STUDIES AND REAL LIFE EXAMPLES

Stories and anecdotes illustrating cultural challenges and successes

Below are a few case studies and real-life examples that illustrate cultural challenges and successes in Fiji:

Integration of indigenous and Christian beliefs

In many Fijian villages, the blending of indigenous and Christian beliefs has led to unique practices and rituals. For instance, in some communities, it is common to see the practice of the traditional kava ceremony alongside Christian prayers. This syncretism showcases Fiji's ability to integrate different beliefs and customs, leading to a harmonious coexistence of traditions.

Interfaith cooperation in times of disaster:

During natural disasters like cyclones, Fiji has witnessed various religious communities coming together to provide aid and support to affected individuals. Hindu temples, Christian churches, and Muslim mosques have all opened their doors as shelters and relief centres for those in need, regardless of their faith. This collaboration illustrates the power of interfaith cooperation and the importance of unity in times of adversity.

Overcoming language barriers in education:

With the diverse linguistic landscape in Fiji, the education system has faced challenges in providing instruction in multiple languages. In response, the Fijian government has implemented policies to ensure that education is accessible in English, Fijian, and Fiji Hindi. By recognizing and addressing the linguistic needs of its population, Fiji has taken steps to create an inclusive and effective educational system.

Collaboration for sustainable development:

Fiji's tourism industry, which is a significant contributor to the nation's economy, relies on the country's pristine natural environment. In recent years, various stakeholders, including indigenous communities, tourism operators, and religious organizations, have come together to promote sustainable development and environmental conservation. These collaborative efforts have resulted in increased awareness and the implementation of eco-friendly practices, highlighting the importance of cross-cultural cooperation in addressing shared challenges.

Navigating cultural differences in the workplace:

A foreign executive working for a multinational company in Fiji found herself struggling to navigate the cultural differences in the workplace. She initially faced difficulties in understanding the indirect communication style and hierarchical structure within the Fijian context. By actively engaging with her Fijian colleagues, learning about their culture, and adapting her communication style, she was able to bridge the cultural gap and foster a more effective and harmonious work environment.

Lessons learned and best practices

The case studies and real-life examples from Fiji demonstrate valuable lessons and best practices that can be applied in various contexts, both within Fiji and beyond. These lessons emphasize the importance of cultural understanding, adaptability, and collaboration.

Embrace cultural diversity

Fiji's ability to integrate different religious beliefs and customs showcases the importance of embracing cultural diversity. By acknowledging and respecting the differences between various cultural groups, a harmonious coexistence can be achieved.

Foster interfaith cooperation

The collaboration of religious communities during times of disaster in Fiji highlights the importance of interfaith cooperation. By working together, these communities can provide support and assistance to those in need, regardless of their faith. This spirit of cooperation can be applied to various challenges, fostering unity and collaboration.

Address linguistic needs

Fiji's commitment to providing education in multiple languages demonstrates the importance of addressing linguistic needs. By recognizing and accommodating diverse language preferences, societies can create more inclusive and effective educational systems.

Collaborate for shared goals

The joint efforts of various stakeholders in Fiji to promote sustainable development and environmental conservation underscore the importance of collaboration in achieving shared goals. By working together, stakeholders can pool their resources, knowledge, and expertise to address common challenges and pursue collective objectives.

Adapt to cultural differences

The experience of the foreign executive in Fiji serves as a reminder of the importance of adapting to cultural differences. By actively engaging with others, learning about their culture, and adjusting one's communication style, individuals can bridge cultural gaps and foster more effective relationships.

Cultivate empathy and cultural intelligence

The various case studies from Fiji emphasize the importance of developing empathy and cultural intelligence. By seeking to understand the perspectives, experiences, and values of others, individuals can better navigate cultural differences and foster more positive and meaningful interactions.

Resources and Further Reading

Books, articles, and websites for further exploration

Books:

- "Fiji: A Travel Survival Kit" by Robyn Jones and Leonardo Pinheiro
- "Fiji and the Fijians: The Islands and their Inhabitants" by Thomas Williams and James Calvert
- "Fiji: An Open-Hearted Culture on the Edge of the Map" by Ian Osborn
- "Culture Smart! Fiji: A Quick Guide to Customs and Etiquette" by Robyn Jones
- "Broken Waves: A History of the Fiji Islands in the Twentieth Century" by Brij V. Lal

Articles:

- "Cultural Identity and Ethnicity in Fiji: A Review of Selected Literature" by Sitiveni Halapua
- "Fiji: A Melting Pot of Cultures" by Roderick Eime
- "Indigenous Fijian and Indo-Fijian Cultural Relations: A Study of the Impact of the Girmit Experience" by Vijay Naidu

Websites:

- Fiji Museum: http://www.fijimuseum.org.fj/
- Tourism Fiji: https://www.fiji.travel/
- UNESCO World Heritage List - Levuka Historical Port Town: http://whc.unesco.org/en/list/1399
- National Archives of Fiji: http://www.archives.gov.fj/
- Fijian Government: https://www.fiji.gov.fj/
- Fiji Times (Newspaper): **https://www.fijitimes.com/**

Language learning resources and cultural organisations

Language Learning Resources

- Transparent Language Online - Fijian: Transparent Language offers a comprehensive language learning course for Fijian, including lessons, activities, and resources to help you learn the language. (https://www.transparent.com/learn-fijian/)

- Fijian for Travelers: A comprehensive guide to learning Fijian, featuring common phrases, essential vocabulary, and pronunciation tips. (https://www.fijian.travel/)

- Pimsleur Fijian: Pimsleur offers an audio-based Fijian language course that focuses on conversational skills and pronunciation. (https://www.pimsleur.com/learn-fijian)

- iTaukei Language and Culture: A Facebook page dedicated to promoting and teaching the iTaukei (Fijian) language and culture. (https://www.facebook.com/iTaukeiLanguage/)

- Memrise - Fijian: Memrise offers a collection of user-generated Fijian language courses that help you learn vocabulary and phrases through interactive games and quizzes. (https://www.memrise.com/courses/english/fijian/)

Cultural Organizations

- Fiji Museum: The Fiji Museum is dedicated to preserving and promoting Fijian history, culture, and heritage. The museum features exhibitions, artefacts, and educational programs that showcase the diverse aspects of Fijian life. (http://www.fijimuseum.org.fj/)

- Fiji Arts Council: The Fiji Arts Council aims to preserve and promote Fijian arts and culture by supporting local artists, organizing cultural events, and providing educational resources. (https://www.facebook.com/FijiArtsCouncil/)

- Fiji National University - College of Humanities and Education: The College of Humanities and Education at Fiji National University offers programs in Fijian language, culture, and history. (https://www.fnu.ac.fj/new/college-of-humanities-education)

- iTaukei Trust Fund Board: The iTaukei Trust Fund Board supports the development of iTaukei culture, heritage, and traditional knowledge by providing funding for various cultural projects and initiatives. (https://www.tltb.com.fj/)

- Fiji Broadcasting Corporation - Radio Fiji One: Radio Fiji One is a Fijian-language radio station that provides news, entertainment, and cultural programming. (https://www.fbc.com.fj/)